BOOKWORMS ANONYMOUS

∞

A Non-Traditional
Book Club for All Readers

Foreword by Patricia Wood,
author of Lottery

Jan Stafford Kellis

ISBN: 1-4392-3513-9
ISBN-13: 9781439235133

Bookworm [book-wurm]: (noun) One obsessed with books, nearly to the point of mania; one compelled to read all words in observation, regardless of context or circumstance; one possessing a preoccupation or fascination with the written word.

This book is dedicated to Bookworms everywhere.
Don't just sit there, read!

Foreword
by Patricia Wood, author of LOTTERY

I write stories that come out of my imagination. There is a vision that formulates in my subconscious of how I want my tale to affect the reader. My goal is always to pull a reader into a world they might not have ever experienced. It is art. It is my art. But just the creation of the story does not mean my art is finished. It takes someone to actually read my story, to bring into the mix his or her experiences. By doing that it will make that particular story unlike any other. Is art finished then? In my opinion no. The final culmination is when readers come together and discuss the piece of art, the novel, the story. It is especially meaningful when the author can be included in the discussion.

As an author when I participate with book clubs it allows me to realize the fruition of my art. To bring it full circle with the reader. Book clubs make literature come alive and it is vibrant with the talking of it, with the urgency one has when one has read a fabulous book. To share? Well that is the basis for it all.

Since my debut novel LOTTERY came out in August 2007 I have talked with over 100 book clubs. We have met on boats, in hotels, in homes, by email, on SKYPE and ichat and via speakerphone. Technology has made this possible — Many book clubs — Many differences in meeting place and style. Each one unique and satisfying to the group members and talking with them has added much insight to my craft as an author.

I am honored to write the foreword to a book about one such unique group and hope you take away the desire to create a group of your own.

Authors will thank you for it because it takes their book from being a solitary pleasure and transforms it by sharing. And that is the point of a good book —

To share it with others.

Much aloha,

Patricia Wood

⁓

Acknowledgments

I composed this book during a long, cold winter while my husband Jason watched the Detroit Red Wings. Situated Indian-style on my recliner with a laptop balanced on my knees with notes and outlines spread across both arms of the chair, I transformed them from scrawled index cards into something I hope people will enjoy reading. Jason kept me supplied with wine and snacks so I wouldn't have to upset my precarious piles of papers, and this is why he deserves to be thanked first. It's also why I now enjoy hockey season.

The Bookworms Anonymous editorial staff earned a close second in thank ranking, for tolerating my repeated requests to read the latest revisions and provide new suggestions. No one complained, not even once. Angie, Jenny Penny, Janelle, Kelly and Stephanie each deserve a generous monetary remuneration for their proofing and editing efforts, but they will receive what I can afford: a copy of the book. My recipe editor, Danielle, formatted the entire recipe section for uniformity and straightforward wording. Thank you!

I must also recognize the Bookworms, the group of women who provided much of the material for this book. They didn't realize it at the time, but I was madly recording details after each meeting! I hope we continue to enjoy swapping books for years to come. Thank you for your enthusiastic support of this project.

Patricia Wood deserves special mention here. When I requested permission to reprint one sentence from her novel *Lottery*, she not only responded promptly and positively, she offered to write a foreword for this book! Her support helped propel me to the finish line. Thank you, Patricia!

Finally, I thank my mom for teaching me how to read, and Angie, for teaching me how to write (I take full responsibility for any errors, though—Angie can only do so much!).

This book is based on a true story; I blended factual characters and events with my somewhat reliable memories to create a work of fact-based fiction. Embellished events and paraphrased conversations appear herein. The meetings portrayed are accurate recreations of typical meetings, and the recipes and menus are authentic.

∾

Life's too short to read bad books.
—Bookworms Anonymous motto

Chapter One

!

The Quiz:
Would you rather read than watch TV?
Is your Christmas wish list mostly books?
Do you look forward to reading mail from QPB?
Is amazon.com your favorite on-line shopping site?
Would you pack two or more books for a 4-day trip?
Do you have more books than bookshelf space?
Do you think of rainy days as "good reading weather"?
If you answered yes to three or more questions,
then please join us!

I first thought someone had diagnosed my compulsive reading disorder and was presenting a cure. Some sort of 12-step program where each book addict must stand before their peers and admit sheepishly: My name is Jan and I'm addicted to reading. I'm sure there's help out there for people like me, but I am comfortable with my affliction. In fact, I like it...the only way to manage compulsive reading is to read. Carrying a book everywhere prevents me from reading cereal boxes, doctor office pamphlets and vacuum cleaner instructions; but those items would suffice in a pinch.

I continued to read the card in my hand and realized it was an invitation—not to a support group or rehab center, but to a small gathering of fellow book addicts. Apparently, the object was to celebrate and share our love of books—not diminish or control our reading habits. Of course I would join such a group! I had a week to prepare for the first meeting.

One would think a week's preparation ample to merely attend, not host, such an event, but I didn't know who else was invited, what I should wear, and most importantly, which books I should bring. Surely other book addicts read better books than I, requiring deep analysis of the symbolism for the true message the author is conveying. My recent divorce severely impacted my book choices. I was reading only light, fluffy stories that didn't require concentration or mental energy, or contain any violence conducive to nightmares. Not that I slept alone. No, in a mere 10 months I'd managed to find a new boyfriend (he was my husband by the time I received the invitation) who moved in within weeks, after falling in love with me and my two daughters at our first meeting. Jason epitomizes Michigan's Upper Peninsula, or Yooper, outdoorsman: he traps, hunts, fishes, owns a construction business, and lives in a flannel shirt and baseball cap. We enjoy many divergent interests, ensuring we never run out of conversation fodder. Although he doesn't like to read, he encouraged me to attend the Bookworms Anonymous meeting.

I wondered if, at the meetings, we would discuss the symbolism of each book, always my least favorite part of English class. I read for entertainment and/or information, but I don't read to unearth the nugget of wisdom buried beneath layers of metaphors, symbols and private demons. If the author has something to say to the reader, she should just say it! Rather than make the reader delve into the far dusty corners of the author's psyche to discover the hidden meaning, she should keep it simple and save English students everywhere from fabricating symbolic clues to appease the teacher. The first time I was assigned a story dissection, I remember asking my mom how I would know which part of the story is sincere and which parts allude to something else. She just shrugged and said, "Crank up your b.s. level. You'll do fine." She was right.

Back to the looming invitation. I settled on wearing jeans and a sweater, quite dressy for functions in the Upper Peninsula, but UP fashion is a topic I'll explore later. The book selection still had me stumped; I felt I would be judged or even ridiculed for reading books without substance. I finally settled on two books, after rejecting approximately twenty sitting on my shelf:

The Persian Pickle Club, by Sandra Dallas

Anna Karenina, by Leo Tolstoy

Surely, these strategic choices would illustrate to the club that although I enjoyed a light read about a quilting bee whose members protected one of their own when she murdered her abusive husband, I could also discuss Tolstoy's classic tale of unrequited love and dismal Russian lives. Thus, I was adequately prepared in case any mention of symbolism came up.

The night of the meeting was cold and dark. Is there any other sort of night in November in Upper Michigan? Janelle's house looked warm and cozy, set above the street at the end of an uphill driveway. At the last minute I left *Anna Karenina* in the car. Surely all bibliophiles have read it already; I would only mention it if pressed for more books. Now I worried I was inadequately prepared, bringing one slim volume to a book club. I anticipated crippling humiliation as I knocked on the door.

Once again, I worried needlessly. My knock was answered promptly and I was ushered into the dining room, seated at the table, and served a glass of wine! A few simple hors d'oeuvres waited on the table, and a glass of ice water at each place setting. Janelle did most of the talking, explaining her ideas for our book club. The basic premise consisted of monthly meetings, each of us bringing the latest books we'd read, and swapping our books with each other. We'd save money, be exposed to more books, and have an excuse to chat and drink wine. There was no down side to this proposal.

The other Charter Members of Bookworms Anonymous included:

Anne, my mom. I've known her since birth, and she taught me to read. My earliest memory of her is my asking her to play a game, but she couldn't because she was reading. I wanted so badly to be an adult so I could sit around and read books! Unable to completely relinquish her teaching career, she's semi-retired and conducts two or three GED preparation classes per week.

Angie, my now retired high school English teacher, whom I've always admired but had never encountered in a social situation. Retirement granted Angie more reading time, and if she isn't reading, she's probably outside gardening, walking, skiing, or riding her bicycle, complete with a flower-bedecked wicker basket. I was honored and thrilled to join a book club with Angie. She and her husband live here in town, and their son and daughter-in-law work at a University downstate.

Jean, another retired woman who has lived here for 30-some years, and is still involved in all kinds of community organizations and events, including playing the piano and directing the choir. She and her husband live in their empty nest, which he has filled with his handmade metal art, both functional and decorative.

Janelle, the hostess, an umpteenth-generation town native who lived in California for several years before returning home with her husband and new son. They now have two sons, three years apart, both in grade school but maturing quickly. Janelle and I share many interests, reading ranking number one on the list. We frequently walk together, wearing the blacktop shiny on our circuitous route around town, talking about everything from diaper rash to dementia and solving the world's problems. Quick with a witty comment or story on a given topic, Janelle is the fastest reader in our bunch and enjoys some local renown as a jewelry maker and an artist, using watercolors and pastels to create portraits and nature scenes.

After our first meeting, two more Bookworms were inducted:

Christine, who designed and built her own octagonal house on a piece of acreage about twenty minutes from town, a single woman with a grown daughter living near Detroit. She plows her own impossibly long driveway, hauls her own wood, and frequently barters with neighbors for various chores or jobs. She was a midwife for many years, and now works part time and spends most of her spare hours kayaking all over the UP.

Jen, my sister, who recently moved back to the UP ready to resume village life. She reads about as much as I do, and although we're seven years apart, we end each other's sentences and often experience simultaneous, identical thoughts. People around town frequently mistake each of us for the other, not noticing the subtle differences in hair color and facial structure. I'm amazed how similar we've become; as children, I sought quiet corners in which to read and listen to the adults' conversation while Jen led a more exciting life, a constant performance she choreographed on the fly, skipping, twirling, climbing trees, skinning knees. Our mother called her Mrs. Jones, often interrupting my reading with the phrase, "Mrs. Jones, *please* sit still for five minutes." I grew up and settled down early, anchoring myself with a baby and husband, but Jen didn't pause for an intermission. She left the UP to study foreign cultures—namely, California and Ohio—eventually discovering she belongs here. She returned and married a local she'd known in high school, and they live next door to his parents. He'll never entertain the idea of moving from the area but he does allow her to rearrange the furniture as often as she wants.

At first glance, we appear a somewhat mismatched bunch. But besides geographical proximity and a love of reading, we enjoy varied interests—skiing, kayaking, snowshoeing, or walking. All of us have children, half of us have been divorced, most of us are currently married, some are retired, and some of us wish we were retired so we could read more. Our ages range from 30 – 70, and most of us have known each other for at least 30 years (including the 30-year-old).

In addition to enjoying similar books, we applaud frugality in a fellow Bookworm; special notice is granted when one finds a book costing less than five dollars worthy of our attention. One of the reasons we chose to form this unusual type of book club is to save money, so we weren't all forced to buy our own copy of a specific book each month. Additionally, we discovered we read books we otherwise would not, based on a fellow Bookworm's endorsement. Our literary circle also provides an important social structure helping each of us through various life trials, including birth, death, caring for elderly parents, scary medical diagnoses, marriage, career changes, new business ventures, and retirement. Rather than gossip at our monthly meetings, we tend to share news about ourselves and our lives as only a few of us socialize outside the Bookworm venue.

Each Bookworm meeting (they are *never* called parties) consists of food, book reviews, and personal insights, starting with food. When we started, we served hors d'oeuvres and wine, then gradually morphed into more complicated hors d'oeuvres and more interesting presentations, eventually upgrading to a proper meal. We start with dinner consisting of a salad, main course and dessert, all vegetarian fare to accommodate our three vegetarians, but we do eat seafood. After our meal we choose someone to begin, and listen to brief reviews of the books she has read since the previous meeting. Progressing around the table round-robin style, we try to make the books we like sound appealing to the other Bookworms. After a book is reviewed, we decide who should read it next (basically, the first one to respond takes it), and the book is passed off. The book will return to a future meeting, to be re-reviewed and passed to another Bookworm. Each of us will take it for a month or more at a time, eventually returning it to its owner.

Everyone else presented more interesting books than I. They actually brought some authors I'd never encountered before; I was surprised and shocked to discover I didn't recognize their names. After all, I was no stranger to the bookstore and library! How did these authors escape my attention? Not only had I never heard of them, the other Bookworms had already read them. And so, I started my Bookworms Anonymous membership at a distinct disadvantage. For the first time since I learned how to read, I had some catching up to do; Barbara Kingsolver and Jane Hamilton became my new favorite authors.

Eight years have passed since our initial meeting and our original septet is still intact. We rarely meet without full attendance, and our meetings are always filled with great food, lots of chitchat, wine, coffee, dessert, and books, books, books. It's divine.

What I expected to be a loss of reading time turned out to increase the volume and enhance the quality of my book selections.

ᢙ

January launches the calendar year, and more importantly, horizontal hold season, in which the reader reclines and reads avidly. Because people are reluctant to brave the weather to visit each other, there's little reason to clean the house. Fewer events mean fewer obligations, especially compared to the previous holiday month. With virtually zero outside maintenance necessary save snow removal, it's perfectly permissible to lie around and read. We also enjoy bright sunny days, great for snowshoeing or cross-country skiing, after which we can drink hot tea and...of course...read.

Home high school basketball games are the only events drawing people from their cozy homes on these frigid nights and this year, our basketball team deserves special mention. We are a class 'D' school, the smallest size in the sports conference, meaning anyone who tries out for a sport is accepted on the team. Like anyone else, we have good years and bad years, but this has been a great year for us. Our boys look fierce on the court, working together like a machine, whipping in and out and back and forth so fast sometimes I don't even see them steal the ball, and suddenly they're racing back down the court and shooting another lay up. A couple of them leap through the air, weightless, twisting and landing with the ball magically swooshing through the net. We're always proud of our kids here, but when they're playing ball like this our pride is palpable. The boys don't belong to themselves or their families when they're on the court; they belong to the spectators, the ragtag cheerleaders who gather on a winter's night to witness another spectacular feat. The band strikes up the school song, prompting the crowd to stand as if on cue and clap in time, whooping as the last note sounds. It's a lively event, and one of the best ways to spend a winter evening in a small town.

This January, with its biting, interminable cold and wonderful basketball game-winning energy, is my turn to host Bookworms. It grows dark around 5:00 p.m., so I punch holes in the snow along our driveway and place a tealight candle in each one, to light the way for my friends as they approach the house. We'll start with a tossed salad, followed by a Spinach Ricotta Tart and ending with Walnut Stuffed Slow-Baked Apples. Satisfying fare for a frigid winter night. I'll brew some decaffeinated coffee to serve with my bottle of red and bottle of white wines, both of which I've been saving for months. The house will be cleaned and candles lit, and a centerpiece will appear on the table. I'll break out the good china for dessert to enhance the presentation. This month, I have a finished mud room and a new painting by my daughter on display. My husband will be ice fishing and my daughters will be occupied in their bedrooms. We'll eat, visit, laugh and carry on, reviewing books and talking about life.

The Bookworms start trooping in just as I finish setting the table. They're all decked out in colorful winter garb, Janelle and Jean in red, my mom in purple, Jen in green, and Christine in a lovely teal coat with fur trim, sporting fancy handmade mittens made from recycled sweaters. Angie is the last one to arrive, muttering to herself about having short legs and not keeping up with the others. Angie portrays "up north" elegance—always dressed in a neat, practical outdoorsy-yet-classy style, she looks fresh off the page of an L.L.Bean catalog.

Books introduced this month:

The Birth House, by Ami McKay

The Whistling Season, by Ivan Doig

Eat, Pray, Love, by Elizabeth Gilbert

The Piano Tuner, by Daniel Mason

Since I was visibly twitching as Angie reviewed Ivan Doig's newest book, she handed it to me before she finished discussing it. I read it in four days. This was easily Doig's best book—I discovered him in a used book store a few years ago, and have since read all of his fiction. Each book has been passed around the Bookworms and received positive reviews. I expect this newest selection, *The Whistling Season*, to earn the Bookworms Stamp of Approval.

This novel, set in rural Montana in 1910, is told by the eldest of three brothers who are being raised on a farm by their widower father who can't cook but has an exceptional command of the English language; I even grabbed the dictionary while reading a couple of his creatively-phrased passages. The boys attend a one-room school, arriving every morning on horseback, sometimes facing backwards. The usual schoolyard shenanigans are handily solved by the new teacher who hails from Minnesota, with a rather hazy past that is eventually explained. I don't want to reveal too much, but Haley's Comet, Latin lessons, death, marriage, betrayal, lies and strength of character are all explored in this book. Ivan Doig's love of language strengthens the story, adding an attractive dimension for word lovers like me.

My stack contains a few returns tonight—books already read and reviewed by at least one other Bookworm, which I've now read and will briefly re-review so the next person can take them. I have one new paperback to share with the group: *Eat Pray Love*, by Elizabeth Gilbert. This book chronicles a year in the author's life, a sort of travelogue of her journey around the world, as she stays for extended periods of time in Italy (where she decompresses and eats), India (where she learns to pray), and Indonesia (where she discovers love), in that order. An intimate look at this woman's life, philosophy, and intense learning experiences, this book deserves shelf space. I read a brief passage marked with a Post-It note to best illustrate the language. I'm sure all Bookworms will enjoy this one, and when I finish reviewing, everyone looks eager to read it so I toss it across the table to Christine.

My mom brought *The Piano Tuner* tonight, and delivers a lukewarm review about a renowned piano tuner who travels to the far reaches of Burma to tune a piano for an eccentric Surgeon-Major in the British Army. His trip to Burma is long and tedious, comprising half the story, and the piano tuner enjoys Burma so much, he stays long after his work is finished. The few interesting sections and graceful turns of phrase are barely enough to maintain consciousness while reading. After reading this thin novel, I agreed with Mom's review: the drawn-out journey and slow action render the story tiresome and (although I hate this word, it applies here) boring.

Mom and I share DNA and a pet peeve: mentally capable people claiming boredom. Uttering the word 'bored' or any of its derivatives was strictly taboo when I was a child. Even a subtle intimation about having nothing to do was immediately met with, "You're smart enough to find something to do. You're not a dullard, are you? Only dull people get bored." Mom's remedy for boredom usually involved chores, so I learned early on to occupy myself by reading. I adopted my mom's habit of grabbing a book every time I leave the house, thus prepared for delays or downtime. Keeping a book readily available transforms inconveniences (such as waiting for the doctor or the tow truck) into reading opportunities. I can't relate to those who waste their doctor's office waiting time fidgeting or playing cell phone games. Obviously, their mothers never taught them to carry a book, effectively handicapping their ability to entertain themselves. Occasionally I forget my book and enter the universe unarmed, unprepared for postponements or contingencies. A niggling anxiety, akin to that felt when a purse or child is forgotten, will infiltrate my mind and compromise my entire day.

After the meeting, we discuss a few books we plan to read or have read in the past, and Sue Monk Kidd's *The Mermaid Chair* is mentioned because it's sitting on my shelf in clear view of the table. Jean has read this book and declares it trash, recalling sex with a Monk and a crazy chair and something about water. We never know what Jean will say—she's 70 years old or so, and possesses a sophistication and grace to which most of us aspire but few attain. Raised on the East Coast, she carries herself with a classy confidence she manages to maintain even when she utters shockingly profane comments. She's one of those people who can do or say anything and it seems appropriate no matter what it is. When I told her about divorcing my first husband, I expected the usual response: lowered head, serious facial expression, the requisite 'I'm sorry'. Not Jean—she jumped up and down and clapped her hands, whooping loudly, celebrating my impending freedom and endorsing my decision, assuring me life was about to get easier. She's the one people call when they need someone to play the piano for a wedding, graduation, funeral or other event. She speaks at various events as well, able to inspire, cajole or comfort the entire audience as the occasion requires. Jean is a rare gem and we're lucky she found our small village and moved here thirty years ago.

Though Jean thought *The Mermaid Chair* was trashy, I read it to find out for myself and was pleased to note there is more to the story than the Monk, the sex and the chair. To me, this was a book about a 40-something woman whose daughter has just left for college, and feels that her marriage is less than exciting. Her mother injures herself, and the woman ends up caring for her mother and finally resolving 30-year-old issues regarding her father's death. In the end she discovers stability is desirable and the former rut looks more like a comfortable groove. It's sort of a late bloomer's coming-of-age story, and contains some important messages. I ended up bringing it to the next Bookworms meeting.

Our meetings follow a pretty loose format: basically we arrive and greet, sit and eat, review and swap books, then schedule our next meeting. Even though we live in a small, isolated town, we sometimes don't cross paths between meetings. Over the years we've scheduled meetings around our work schedules, volunteer schedules, vacations and other events. There are seven of us, so if two or more can't attend a meeting we reschedule. We've been known to cut vacations short, hire babysitters, and even send our husbands to the bar in order to attend a BA meeting (or host one, in the case of the husband at the bar).

Since our meetings revolve around books, the book reviews are critical. One must sum up the pertinent details regarding character, story line or plot, and entice other Bookworms to read the book. The challenge is to relate enough details to interest another Worm without spoiling any plot twists or revealing a surprise ending. Some book reviews consist of one phrase, immediately inspiring everyone to read it: "This is Anna Quindlen's new one," is enough to incite a friendly riot as we all reach for the book. A review of Kazuo Ishiguro's *Never Let Me Go* was slightly longer, and cryptically phrased: "This story takes place at a private school in England. It's bizarre and disturbing. That's all I can say." Other book reviews are laborious pleas rarely resulting in any interested takers: "This subject is something everyone should know about; it's written in newspaper article style, like a documentary, about World War II and the heinous acts committed by both US soldiers and the Japanese." After hearing this off-putting review, we each gaze toward the ceiling waiting for the moment to pass. Most book reviews, though, contain a brief synopsis of the plot and/or characters without revealing too much. Eight years of accumulated Bookworm history allows us to accurately predict who will like a given book; sometimes a book review is aimed at only one or two Bookworms, with the (usually correct) assumption the others won't want to read it.

After we arrive and greet, then sit and eat, we enjoy some small talk while we sip our wine, water or decaf coffee—I usually have all three beverages, sentinels lined up along the top of my place mat, protecting me from dehydration; then the hostess will ask someone to begin. We all retrieve stacks of books from our bags and prepare to review our latest reads. We pour more wine and settle in, listening to reviews of new books and of those still making their way around the group.

With so much great material, the book discussion is a long one. Our conversation finally returns to mundane matters such as dental work and new movie releases. No one is eager to leave the warm house for the icy trek to the frosty car, which won't warm up until it arrives home. Someone finally stands up, stashing her books, and we hastily schedule the next meeting. Everyone troops out the door and drives away, the candles along the drive glowing weakly in the inky night.

Jan's Menu

Lentil Pate*

Spinach & Ricotta Tart*

Fresh Fruit

Walnut-Stuffed Apples*

Coffee * Merlot * Chardonnay * Ice Water

*recipes included in Appendix C

"It's hard to turn pages with my mittens on."
"The snow keeps ruining my book!"

Chapter Two

The sun shines with such intensity in midwinter, the snow doubling the effect by bouncing sparkles around and banishing the memories of January's gloom, sunglasses are required to avoid blindness. This season is best witnessed from inside, as the thermometer hovers around zero and the slightest breath of wind causes my whole body to ache. Enter book shuffling, a sport most enjoyed in the winter when we read more and surrender to our hibernating tendencies. My bookcase is organized first by type of book, then alphabetically by author, except the books I haven't yet read, which are in the order I plan to read them. For instance, the bottom shelf contains reference books—everything from gardening to cooking, old text books, wine making, dog training, hair cutting, cross stitch, sewing and scrapbooking, almost all of my interests represented. All reference books on the middle shelves are language oriented: dictionaries, thesauri, writing style guides, punctuation guides, composition exercises, and books featuring an irreverent approach to writing such as *Woe is I* and *Eats, Shoots and Leaves*. The remaining middle shelf real estate is reserved for fiction books I've saved, ostensibly to re-read. So far, the only books I've ever re-read were *Gone With the Wind, The Thorn Birds*, and *Grease*. I was still in high school and going through an annual re-reading phase, reading the same three books each year in addition to my regular reading. I haven't re-read anything since, and yet I am compelled to maintain a small library of possible future rereads in case I ever run completely out of reading material, a highly improbable, quite ghastly scenario.

The top book shelf hosts my Bookworm books: an ever-evolving, revolving selection of books I purchased intending to pass around the club, and books I have borrowed from fellow Worms. This portion of the bookcase is where all book shuffling action occurs.

Book shuffling is not a nervous habit or an anxiety-ridden second guessing battle with myself, it's a methodical book ranking procedure to ensure I read the books in optimal order, guaranteeing each book is fully enjoyed and relished. After reading a long, complicated novel like *I Know This Much Is True* by Wally Lamb, it's nearly impossible to tackle another one as lengthy or richly written immediately. Using light fluffy books, such as those written by Lorna Landvik or Helen Fielding, as the filler between two 'heavy' tomes greatly enhances all three books. The fun, fluffy sandwich books provide a restful interlude for our minds, allowing us to recalibrate and prepare for the next serious bite. Some books are shuffled and reshuffled several times before they are ever read; this usually occurs when the current book isn't as stimulating as expected and I'm desperately slogging through it, hoping the next one will restore my equilibrium. After reading an all-consuming, reality-altering novel, it's impossible to choose the next book and I resort to asking my spouse, child or dog to pick one for me. Although less calculated, this method works when the decision is overwhelming.

ᦓ

Winter is firmly established now, delivering snow, subzero temperatures, wind and icy sleet at whim. Yesterday's storm deteriorated my driveway to its typical winter condition: non-navigable for the average motorist. This will last from mid-winter through spring, which constitutes roughly 1/3 of the calendar. Before we finished building our house, the rain washed out our driveway causing the delivery truck loaded with roof trusses to remain at the bottom of the hill. It's not even a hill, really, but a short little rise, just enough to render anyone without four-wheel-drive immobile or, worse, stuck in the soft shoulder. If my husband Jason had a dollar for every time he's driven or pushed someone out of our driveway, we could afford to pave it and we wouldn't have this problem.

The entire driveway, from the edge of the road to the edge of the garage pad, is only 250 feet long. Starting with a shallow dip, it gradually rises to the height of the house on top of the ridge, about 25 feet higher than the lowest point. It's straight and has a ditch on each side of the low part, the rise edged by a green wall of crowded cedar trees on the right side and by our front yard on the left. It doesn't look like much of a challenge, but the number of vehicles this driveway sucks in belies its appearance.

We repaired the driveway after finishing the house, reasoning the trouble was limited to heavy delivery trucks. New gravel was added, leveled, and graded, and we figured our driveway debacle had ended. Since then, we've had a FedEx truck, the wrecker (hired to extricate the FedEx truck, ultimately needing an excavator to remove the wrecker), UPS van, school bus, and numerous cars, trucks and vans stuck on ice, wedged sideways across the driveway, or lodged deep in the snowbank on either side. Once we had two vehicles stuck simultaneously, one heading down and one heading up, when a friend of ours slid off on the way up in her van then used one of our vehicles to try to extract it, sliding into the snow on the opposite side. We could have sold tickets, as we put on quite a circus pulling everyone out with the wrecker stuck again on the ice, tires spinning uselessly. At the first snowflake, we advise people to stay at the bottom of our driveway, warning them about the others who have gone before; but its benign appearance causes people to think we're spinning urban legends until they get halfway up and have to ask for help.

Although we've made no financial gains extricating people from the driveway, we've earned the Yooper equivalent: free beer, just as good as money, or even better, since we don't have to drive to town and trade the money for beer. This is the first thing people offer when we decline money; the average conversation goes something like this:

"Thanks for pulling me out. I know you warned me, but it didn't look like much trouble so I tried it anyway. What do I owe you?"

"Oh, nothing. Don't worry about it."

"Well, what kind of beer do you drink?"

"Busch Light."

Within two days, we discover a fresh case of Busch Light sitting on the kitchen counter. Maybe we should somehow boobytrap the driveway so it's difficult to navigate in the summer, too, since that's when beer tastes the best.

Luckily, we already met at my house this season; it's my mom's turn to host Bookworms tonight. We can all park on the street during the meeting, since Mom lives on the main street in town and no one will be out after 5:00 pm on a Sunday evening this time of year.

As we file into my mom's house for our meeting, everyone comments on her recently redecorated dining room. Compliments on her paint and wall border choices are interspersed with friendly greetings, smiles, and the scrape and clatter of chairs as we settle ourselves at the table. Mom makes an excellent lentil casserole, which she's serving this evening. The cold is bitter and it takes some serious hot food to restore proper core body temperatures. Lentil casserole is just the ticket, and accompanied by her mozzarella tomato salad, it's more than I anticipated yet just what I'd hoped for. Cream cheese sugar cookies follow the main course, compelling all of us to request the recipe. Mom is always trying recipes from the backs of various packages, enhancing and tweaking until the results are perfect.

Tonight we discuss one of our favorite authors: Carol Shields, a prolific Canadian author, who, in our collective opinion, is incapable of writing a bad book. As a rule, we Bookworms don't read romance novels, even tending to skim through romantic passages as they seldom add to the story. We made an exception for Carol Shields, and in consideration of her well-established ranking on our list of favorite authors we are reading *The Republic of Love*, a slim work I stumbled upon at a used book store. I always check for my favorite authors in the stacks, and am occasionally rewarded. The general consensus about this particular romance, in which the two main characters don't even meet until halfway through the novel, is that it's good because it's a Carol Shields, despite its nauseatingly romantic theme.

As usual after reading a Carol Shields book, one of us pipes up with "It's not as good as the *Stone Diaries*". We all nod knowingly, recalling the *Stone Diaries* was our introduction to her prose. My futile mental search for information about the *Stone Diaries* is interrupted by my mom, asking, "Does anyone really *remember* the *Stone Diaries*? I recall thinking it was a great book, but I can't recollect the story line, characters, or setting." The room is still as we swivel our heads back and forth, waiting for someone to share something relevant about the *Stone Diaries*. No one does. It seems we read and enjoyed a great book and benchmarked it against others while forgetting it entirely. A brief discussion of memory loss ensued.

Memory loss aside, we all agree it's okay to forget a book after reading it. One is removed from reality for the moment, and isn't that the point of reading? To learn, and to remove oneself. At least we all remember it was a great book. Angie appoints Janelle to reread it and report back to the group.

This month, a diverse selection is offered:

> *Fly Boys*, by James Bradley
> *Your Oasis on Flame Lake*, by Lorna Landvik
> *When Madeline Was Young*, by Jane Hamilton
> *Booking Passage*, by Thomas Lynch
> *The White*, by Deborah Larsen
> *Truth & Beauty: A Friendship*, by Ann Patchett

Jane Hamilton is one of the Bookworm favorites; we've read everything she's published, and we're always delighted with her prose. She creates such vivid, realistic characters, we feel as if we know them, and when we can't recall the name of a Hamilton novel we can usually evoke the characters and plot line. This month's Hamilton selection, presented by Janelle, is about a young wife who survives a bicycle accident with severe head trauma and regresses to the mental level of a six-year-old. Her husband ends up divorcing Madeline and marrying her nurse, but Madeline remains in their care. They raise a family along with Madeline, who never improves but is always happy and content. Hamilton relates this unlikely story line in such a straightforward manner, it is a pleasurable read with a unique theme.

Another favorite author of mine, Ann Patchett, wrote a powerful profile of her best friend in the book *Truth & Beauty: A Friendship.* It's a deep exploration of the personality and character of her friend, Lucy Grealy, a fellow writer who sustained many surgeries to remove cancer from, and reconstruct, her face. A non-fictional account of Ann's and Lucy's lives as they intertwined, and Lucy's struggles with self-confidence, public acclaim for her writing, and drug addictions, this book describes the deep faith Ann had in Lucy, and the trials their friendship endured. After reading it, I learned a bit more by researching online. This book will live with me for a long time.

I brought a Lorna Landvik tonight, a great sandwich book perfect for reading after *Truth & Beauty.* Landvik writes light, enjoyable novels, and *Your Oasis on Flame Lake* portrays two Minnesotan families typical in appearance, with just enough drama to keep the reader entertained. The characters take turns narrating the story chapter by chapter through several plot twists. My favorite character was Dick Lindstrom, the husband and father who wants to open a night club in his basement. He's in love with his wife, even after discovering her transgressions, and he allows his ten-year-old daughter to dissect dead animals to further her interest in veterinary medicine. It's not great literature, but I enjoyed it for its characters and entertainment value.

Two of Landvik's other novels, *Angry Housewives Eating BonBons* and *Welcome to the Great Mysterious*, previously toured the Bookworms Anonymous group and earned rave reviews. *Angry Housewives* examines a women's book club, wherein the members read the same book at the same time then meet to discuss it. Their group actually prepared meals related to each book, complete with theme decorations and place settings. The women's personal struggles are shared with the group, and the reader gets to know each one intimately through Landvik's use of revolving narrators. *Welcome to the Great Mysterious* features a declining Broadway star who answers a frantic call by her sister to come and care for her nephew with Down Syndrome while his parents travel to Italy for a month-long vacation. Predictably, the Broadway star is jarred back to reality after being plunked down in the middle of a rural Minnesota winter. She finds a love interest and reconnects with her childhood when she rediscovers an old scrapbook she and her sister had made as children. The scrapbook is full of life's biggest questions, answered by their parents and grandparents, constructed of cereal box cardboard and glued photos and decorations. The description of the scrapbook and its messages make this book worth reading.

The Worms are getting restless at this stage of the meeting, and Mom starts clearing the table. Tonight we met in the front room, as she has repurposed the room once again. Her house boasts a rich history, beginning more than 110 years ago when two sisters ventured into the woods on what is today's main street and built two houses side by side. Indoor plumbing was added later, creating a tiny passageway between the original building and the 'new' bathrooms. The passageway is so narrow, in order to move a kitchen chair from the front of the house to the back, one must go outside! It has three kitchens and two bathrooms from its brief incarnation as a boarding house, and features small rooms with high ceilings. With no foundation, it rests on strategically placed cinder blocks and stacks of wood, right on the ground, with a fifteen-inch crawl space.

�◡

Everyone worries; it's human nature to worry. We worry about being late, looking foolish, saying the wrong thing, offending or inconveniencing others. We worry about getting enough sleep, eating healthy foods, exercising enough, and teaching our children right from wrong. We worry about the economy, the climate, fashion trends, our culture, aging too fast, not aging at all, global warming, overpopulation, and of course, we worry about worrying too much. I've always known my grandma worried more than the average person. Her level of worry was evident in the way she fussed over everyone, constantly fretting over the dangers of traffic, poison ivy, and insufficient yogurt intake. After spending time with Grandma, I ridiculed her worrying. I scoffed at worry, belittled it, and swore I'd never worry like she did. What a ridiculous waste of time, this worrying! Until one day when I was ten, and my mom didn't come home. She was supposed to arrive at 6:00 pm, driving from Grandma's place. It was a six-hour drive on a two-lane highway with at least one section under construction at any given time. I knew the thirty minute rule: if a person will be more than thirty minutes late, it is courteous to call and alert the person waiting. The waiter is required to wait thirty minutes before starting to worry about the one running late. I waited the requisite thirty minutes to commence worrying: it was a fine summer day, but it was a long drive on a road known for semi-truck accidents, rogue log truck mishaps, and long dull stretches that induced driver fatigue. I waited an additional fifteen minutes, contemplating various improbable scenarios, pacing the kitchen floor to the rhythm of the second hand. I'm not sure where Dad was; it must have been a work day. I finally called Information, chatting with the operator while she retrieved my requested numbers. Still no sign of Mom, now an hour late. A full one-sixth of the entire trip time! Surely I had followed protocol, doubling the thirty-minute courtesy time. I grimly started dialing. I didn't even consider letting Grandma know Mom was late; she'd have been catatonic with worry! No, this was something I could handle on my own. I first contacted hospitals and police stations nearest to Grandma's, and worked my way east. I calmly explained to each person my mother was uncharacteristically, drastically late and I was checking to see if there had been any accidents. I was ending my last call when Mom strolled in. She was perfectly fine, but had left Grandma's an hour later than planned. "Why didn't you just call Grandma?" It sounded logical when she said it. "I didn't want her to worry," was my inadequate reply.

I was diagnosed twenty years later, on a beautiful summer day during a casual conversation with a virtual stranger over margaritas on her front porch. "You have RIS," she said, confident and apologetic in her analysis. At my eyebrow raise, she continued, "Runaway Imagination Syndrome. Basically, it's like when someone is thirty minutes late, you start planning their funeral. After all, why else would anyone be late? Every mother has it."

What a relief the diagnosis afforded! It became much easier to recognize the instant my worry exploded into incapacitating dementia. Now whenever my imagination grows legs and starts running, it is comforting to realize I'm not just a nutty worrier like Grandma; I have a syndrome! A bona fide medical reason for my crazy behavior.

My close friends and family all know I suffer from RIS. Some of them are similarly afflicted, so we sometimes remind each other: "return my messages and emails so I know you're still alive, before my RIS flares up!" At least it isn't contagious. The best way to control RIS? Divert attention and keep the mind busy. Read!

Anne's Menu

Mozzarella Tomato Basil Salad*

Lentil Casserole*

Cheese & Crackers

Cream Cheese Cookies*

Coffee* Pinot Noir* White Zinfandel* Ice Water

*recipes included in Appendix C

Never settle for less than fabulous.

Chapter Three

We're famous for our weather. Upper Peninsula winters are renowned for their length, low temperature, immense amounts of snow, and length. Did I mention how long they are? Eventually, we reach the end of human toleration for winter. Everything winterish we loved (okay, endured) during the first three months of winter are now trite, and we're tired. Our spirits keep pace with the temperature, staying low on average with the occasional spike on a nice day. Speaking of spirits, this is a banner time for the bar as snowmobile season drags on and the locals desperately drink their way toward spring, a distant memory at best and a cruel, taunting illusion at worst.

I combat the weather's malicious effects by practicing yoga every morning and snowshoeing two or three times per week. Yoga does wonders for my overall well-being, like a daily attitude adjustment wrapped up in a physical improvement. My stomach looks the same, but feels firmer. On the inside, anyway. It's still disturbingly puddinglike when I poke at it. I don't dwell on this development (or should I call it an *un*development?) as I'm afraid to invite any interior negativity to join that already provided by the calendar and barometer.

It's the desperation, the journey through toleration and beyond, that affects people. We call it Cabin Fever; the media and medical types call it Seasonal Affect Disorder. Simulating the worst episode of PMS, multiplied by ten, it's the legendary reason for going completely crackers by candlelight. The sun sets by 5:00 every afternoon, and by 6:00 or 7:00 the town appears abandoned: blinds are pulled, cars are parked, all three streets are free of wandering dogs. Darkness and isolation combine to reveal our worst personalities and our lowest potentials, triggering a few acts of minor insanity every year at this time. Nothing too earth-shattering, merely drunken adventures involving driving a vehicle into the bar and shooting at the animals mounted on the walls, or wearing a pair of moon boots and a grass skirt to dance on the tables, or spending an entire unemployment check in one night buying rounds for the regulars. Witnessing these performances can cause its own disorder, although there is no medical term for it. Our town is small, but we'd probably be able to keep a psychologist busy if one ever opened shop. Of course, it would be impossible to maintain anonymity while driving to and from appointments, in a town where turn signals are superfluous because everyone already knows where everyone else is going.

To fully understand and appreciate the size of our town and the magnitude of information flowing freely about each resident, stop in the local restaurant and listen to the coffee klatschers for a little while. They'll discuss which spouses are unfaithful, which dogs aren't being fed properly, and who has the most unacknowledged illegitimate children.

∾

No matter how many books I read in a winter month, I'll probably never match my grandmother's rate of one book per day. She always was an energetic reader, choosing everything from Jackie Collins to Steven King, and when she became housebound we started bringing her every large print library book we could find. I think she read every large print book in the small niche at the library at least three times, regardless of subject. We just kept methodically cycling our way though the stacks, grabbing all new arrivals and a few of the regular selections each week. At this stage of her life, Gram's world was reduced to two rooms, and our weekly visits became her favorite events. We always brought books, presenting each separately to prolong our conversation, and we were there for purely social reasons—no baths, no blood pressure checks, no medical indignities. Since she was nearly deaf, I would write comments on her note pad and she would respond verbally. Occasionally the conversation would lull and she'd sift through my jottings and revive our chat with fresh observations. Gram lived to be 98—nearly 99—and until the final five years of her life, she was constantly on the go. I would call her when I was ten minutes away and she would come trotting out and hop in my car, ready to go shopping and do lunch. She firmly ignored her worsening hearing loss; it was unladylike and undignified to acknowledge infirmity or handicap. One of the funniest moments

I recall occurred at a restaurant as we were studying our menus. I glanced up at Gram and said, "You look very nice today, Gram." To which she confidently replied "Roast beef sandwich."

Reading a large number of books presents a memory challenge: even at the tender age of a-lot-younger-than-98, I can usually recall a title and/or author, but it's becoming increasingly difficult to remember every story line and sometimes I don't even recall whether or not I liked a book. Enter the book journal: mine provides tidy, satisfying statistics about my reading habits. I note the month in which I read the book, the title and author, and whether it was fiction or non-fiction. Each book is rated, allowing me to tell at a glance which ones were worth reading. Friends are always requesting book recommendations, and it's nearly impossible to conjure a title or author on command unless it's a recent read. Now I simply refer to my book journal and email a list of favorites.

Angie signs her books as she finishes them, scrawling a sideways signature with the date underneath. Some people note in their planners when they start or finish a book; some keep a log in the planner to organize their reading lists year by year. Recording books, authors, dates and ratings lends a sense of accomplishment, a sort of checking-off of a task on a list, and is interesting to peruse months or years later. After time, reading patterns emerge; if one were so inclined, reading habits could be graphed to provide a visual peaks-and-valleys wave (just kidding—this is too obsessive, even for me!). An avid reader may develop an appreciation for winter's downtime after observing their reading habits.

‍‌‌‌

Jenny Penny (Jen to most people) is my younger sister and the hostess for tonight's meeting. She's seven years younger than I, so naturally when we were younger I was the teacher and she the student during our classroom re-enactments. My mom has kept a paper Jenny turned in to me during one of our school sessions, on which I had written: *Jenny's work is sloppy, too sloppy.* I have questioned the negative effect this may have had, but despite my relentless instruction and criticism during her formative years, she managed to grow into a beautiful, brave woman with a wry wit. She is decision challenged, though, and I can't help but wonder if she still hears my critical voice every time she tries to choose which sweater to wear or which car to buy. She's pregnant with her first child, obsessing about the name. It must be a strong name, a boy's name, and of course her husband must agree to the name. Jen, having one of the most popular names on the planet, is determined to give her son a less common name. It must be his own name, not shared with anyone we know, yet not too outlandish as she doesn't want him to be bullied and teased on the playground. The initials must not create or suggest an inappropriate word; diminutive forms of the name must be considered with a juvenile attitude to prevent it from being bastardized. She asked me last week if choosing the name is more difficult than labor. I said yes. Labor is temporary; his name will last his whole life. My sister also suffers from RIS, and is deeply concerned about labor and delivery. Several people have regaled her with their horror stories, the point of which I'll never know. Why scare her now, when she has no recourse?

Tonight we are gathered at Jen's to admire her incongruously large belly and enjoy each other's company near the end of an intolerably long winter season. It's difficult to fit 7 people around one table in a 1960's house trailer sporting reflectors on its exterior ends, but Jenny not only managed it, she created quite a cozy atmosphere with candlelight and background music. The trailer, thankfully, is a temporary abode, making it tolerable and even a source of humor—the 70's paneling, the old crank-out windows, the formerly shag carpet, all provide much fodder for ridicule. Jen and her husband have purchased a sixty-acre parcel across the road and are madly sketching house plans, studying books, listing requirements and compromising to reach agreement by this spring. I think they've used more eraser than pencil on their house plans so far, but it's clear the house will feature elements unheard of in the trailer: closets, large windows, window seats, reading nooks and niches and library shelves.

We remove our winter gear and arrange ourselves around the table, chattering and pouring wine, while Jen ladles out her vegetarian chili and passes the corn bread around. Cooking is not one of her main interests, but she always presents a great meal. The menu she chose on this bitter, barren night is cheery and comforting. Apricot Whip is a perfect dessert, light and evocative of summer.

Tonight's meeting features tall stacks of books, as is typical of our winter meetings. As each Bookworm arranges her impressive pile of books near her place at the table, the others murmur respectfully with oohs, aahs, and comments on each other's voracious reading habits. When someone boasts, "I had the flu!" We all congratulate her and wish we had been likewise struck, to allow some uninterrupted, guilt-free reading time.

Some of this month's featured selections include:

The Magician's Assistant, by Ann Patchett

The Last Anniversary, by Liane Moriarty

The Bright Forever, by Lee Martin

Not Quite What I Was Planning: Six-Word Memoirs by Writers Famous & Obscure

A Spot of Bother, by Marc Haddon

Two Rivers, by T. Greenwood

Angie brought *Soul Mountain,* but her review handily dissuades us from even attempting to read it. This is a relief, as we are all taking more books than usual due to the large number in circulation. Angie's reviews are notoriously negative. It's rather comical as she presents a book, even one she likes, with a less-than-positive light. "I'm glad I read this book," she'll say, "although it doesn't have proper punctuation and the margins are narrow, so you probably won't like it. It was the only book I took on vacation, and we didn't stop at a bookstore. I read the whole thing. It's rather disturbing, about a girl who is murdered, but then you find out in the end that it's her brother. Oh, I shouldn't have said that! I should *not* have said that. There are plenty of other surprises in the book. Well, just take my word for it, you'll probably enjoy this book." By this time, three or four hands are stretched toward Angie so she just places the book in the nearest one and continues with the next review.

Janelle brought a British novel, *A Spot of Bother,* which she reviews in British style, with dry witty comments and downplaying all drama. Basically, the story is about a neurotic English family. One wonders if the neuroticism is a competition—the father seems to be winning, if it is. George has recently retired, and he and his wife Jean have two grown children and are struggling to live alone together again. Jean seeks solace in her lover David, a former co-worker of George's, and when George witnesses their coupling he is appalled by the sight of two old, wrinkled bodies in his bed, not even recognizing his wife for several moments. Jean and George's son and daughter, Jamie and Katie respectively, have troubles of their own: Jamie is gay and reluctant to commit to his partner, while Katie is a divorced single mother about to marry someone she's not sure she loves. George's imagination frequently spirals out of control, resulting in hilarious incidents and injuries and causing his entire family to believe he has gone mad. Convinced he's dying of cancer after being diagnosed with eczema, he attempts a surgical procedure to remove the "tumor" and ends up in the hospital. The author keeps it semi-dry to maintain maximum entertainment throughout. I grab the book to read it next, recalling I enjoyed his earlier work.

Marc Haddon's other book, *The Curious Incident of the Dog in the Nighttime*, is a must-read told from the perspective of an autistic child assigned to write a book. He chooses to write it about the murder of a neighborhood pet, thereby solving the crime in the process. The reader gains an understanding of autism and what it's like from the inside.

Janelle also brought *Letting Loose the Hounds* and she holds it up for all to view. "This is the book I emailed you about, ladies—I was so excited to find another book by Brady Udall. Remember, his other one was awarded the Stamp of Approval?" We're nodding dutifully, recalling *The Miracle Life of Edgar Mint*, which starts out describing a kid whose head was just run over by a car and doesn't slow down from there. "I bought this in a flurry without doing my homework. It's a volume of short stories! I can't believe I spent good money on short stories."

"That happens to me about once every two years," I commiserate, recalling my triumphant purchase of Elizabeth Gilbert's *Pilgrims* only to discover it's a collection of short stories. "The short stories should be more clearly labeled. Book cover designs can be misleading. It's like a flim flam scheme."

"You were bamboozled," says Jen.

"Hoodwinked!" I can't resist chiming in.

"Have you read any of these Udall stories?" Angie asks Janelle.

"I read a few and they were good; I'd rather read full-length novels right now, so I'm shelving it unless someone wants to take it. I may go back to it later. Much later."

"I'll take it. Sometimes I need something short between books, and I'll read a short story if I finish a book in the evening so I can begin a new full-length one the next day. It'll take me a while to get through it that way, but if you don't mind..."Angie trails off, already gripping the book.

"Not a problem; take your time." Janelle is glad to temporarily relinquish the story collection.

My stack includes a few good reads, so I start out with *The Last Anniversary*, by an Australian author. The cover art drew me to the book; I tend to judge books by their covers, although I've read many great books with poorly-designed covers and a few lousy books with beautifully-designed covers. This particular cover was a pencil drawing depicting a small island with houses, trees, and paths crisscrossing every which way. It looked like a place I'd want to visit, so I dove right in.

The entire story takes place on Scribbly Gum Island, a tiny island and tourist attraction off the coast of Australia reached by private ferry. The island itself is home for the entire Gordon family, who take turns conducting tours of the Jack and Alice Munro House, famous for its lack of inhabitants. It seems Jack and Alice disappeared forever one morning leaving behind their infant daughter, a partially completed crossword puzzle, some bloodstains on the kitchen floor, and a marble cake in the oven. Two young neighbor girls discovered the crying infant, and ended up naming her Enigma and raising her in their home. The mystery entranced the nation; everyone was eager to see the scene for themselves, painstakingly recreated each day by the tour guide on duty. The marble cake must be prepared from scratch daily and placed in the oven at exactly the right time to be removed during the tour, and the story must be recited verbatim as written by Connie, the clan matriarch. When Connie dies, she leaves her house to her grandson's ex-girlfriend, who develops a crush on her ex-boyfriend's cousin's husband (confused yet?) when the cousin is experiencing postpartum-triggered depression. The book's title refers to the annual celebration of Enigma's rescue; she is now a grandmother, and this will be the last anniversary.

I don't want to ruin the mystery here, so I'll just say the disappearance has a perfectly plausible explanation that may or may not be figured out before it's revealed in the book. The characters are endearing, easily remembered long after the final page is read. Janelle adds it to her stack.

The next book in my stack is completely different: *Not Quite What I Was Planning* is a collection of memoirs, each one only six words, by various authors. One can flip it open to a random page or read it straight through; either way, pausing to consider the more poignant or humorous memoirs will enhance the whole book and its messages. Using punctuation wisely, six words can stretch to encompass a lifetime, a personality, a culture, a vacation, an event or a personal creed. It's impossible to discuss this book without counting words and developing a new appreciation and respect for brevity. After I read a few samples out loud, we compose our own memoirs:

Mother too soon; unprepared for adulthood.

Books galore, reading more, never bored.

Yooper girl, happily married. Baby ripe!

Winter stretches long, stealing summer time.

Blessed with boys; constant noise, toys.

Never settle for less than fabulous.

Life is wondrous: brief and divine.

The six-word memoir garnered the attention of teachers nationwide from fourth grade through college, so I loaned my copy to my daughter's English teacher and she assigned the class to write their own memoirs. We'll be able to read them at the Fine Arts Fair this spring, where they'll be displayed alongside drawings, paintings and wood shop projects created by our students.

My mom appears excited about her discovery as she begins presenting *Two Rivers* by T. Greenwood. "This is an engaging story—it's about one man's life so far, and the author switches timeframes with each chapter. The interesting thing here is that T. Greenwood is female and she relates this story in the first person from the perspective of a widower raising his daughter alone. His name is Harper Montgomery, if you please. It takes place in Vermont, and when a train derails in their small town, he takes in a pregnant black teen. Remember, this is Vermont— she's quite noticeable amidst the pale residents, but she's so bright and friendly, people accept his lame explanations when he introduces her. I'll let the next Worm to read it discover for herself what happens. There's a lot in here, from insanity to civil rights to racism and overcoming racism. I think everyone will enjoy it." By now, six hands are reaching toward her to take the book. She hands it off to Christine.

Our discussion turns to spring break plans and past vacations, debates about which facets of vacations are the best (Shopping? Sightseeing? Dining out? Sleeping in? Reading. Definitely reading.), and which destinations are our favorites. More wine is poured, more dreams are shared, more troubles disappear. Enjoying the challenge of word economy, we sum up our vacation plans in exactly six words.

We are comfortable here in the cozy little room, and the meeting lasts until nearly 9:00 as we discuss whether or not spring will arrive this year. It's still too early for spring to debut, of course, but we all crave a promise, a glimpse, a mere suggestion of winter's reprieve. The snow crunches underfoot as we leave, laden with books for the coming month and awed by the stars overhead, counting the words that come to mind, striving for a six-word description of the evening.

Jen's Menu

Vegetarian Chili*

Corn Bread

Cheese & Crackers

Apricot Whip*

Coffee * Shiraz * Riesling * Ice Water

*recipes included in Appendix C

Pedal fast! The library closes in 20 minutes!

Chapter Four

Every Yooper I know suffers from the UP strain of Geographic Identity Disorder. Yes, we actually derive part of our identity from our superior geographic location, pitying the souls unlucky enough to live downstate or, worse, in a completely generic place such as Kansas. The official definition of GID is: the need to live in Michigan's Upper Peninsula in spite of perpetual economic depression, lack of shopping opportunities, and a barbarian climate so we can work two jobs, buy in bulk, and master the art and fashion of layering to survive subzero temps. We scoff at trolls—those who live below the bridge—and take pride in our work trucks and callused hands. Up here, prestige cannot be earned. Our lineage is our status symbol, and the more generations we can trace back, the higher our social standing. It's a tough place to move to, for someone who wants to belong. The advantages of living up here are infinite, and although I cannot list them all, here are my top five: no violent crime; fresh air; locking doors and vehicles isn't necessary; no earthquakes, hurricanes, deadly snakes or spiders, etc.; and there's always something to talk about...the weather. It's been said that if the weather is unpleasant, just wait fifteen minutes. It'll change.

So, those of us raised here suffer from GID, making it difficult to survive other cultures. Many Yoopers (those lucky enough to live in the UP) have ventured downstate and beyond, only to return with horrific stories of multi-lane highways jammed with people they don't recognize and air they can *see*. They return here with little or no prospect of a job, and hire on at the wood mill or local bar to keep food on the table. After the post-traumatic stress dissipates, they're able to function again and that glassy look leaves their eyes. They tell us stories of life on the outside: people wearing suits to work, driving two-wheel drive trucks or cars, men wearing jewelry...it's all very foreign and unsettling, and requires several beers to even contemplate such a dismal existence. It's rare to see a man without a baseball cap and a flannel shirt around here, everyone has four-wheel drive, and for men, wedding rings are optional and there is no other type of jewelry.

When meeting someone from Michigan, one can expect them to indicate where they live—everyone with two hands always has a map of Michigan with them. Not so with the other states—location becomes vague, with hazy, inaccurate directionals: the southwest corner of Nebraska; the top of Idaho. I always picture the sun shining in these generic places, but otherwise they look pretty grim. It seems like a person could lose themselves completely, living in Iowa or Vermont. It must be more difficult to remember where one lives when one can't demonstrate the two peninsulas, then point to one's hometown. The only other place in the world remotely comparable is Italy, but even then high-heeled boots would be required to indicate location.

Our remote location appeals to travelers, and the Chamber of Commerce and local business owners are attempting to transform our town into a tourist destination rather than a place people merely pass through. We have overnight accommodations, a couple of restaurants, churches, bars, a sporting goods store and hardware store, and a new gift shop. The gift shop is owned by six women (three of us are also Bookworms: myself, Janelle and Angie) each with her own lines of favorite products. We take turns working in the store and maintaining the grounds. Situated in a prime location on the main street in an old two-story house, our store boasts a shiny new custom-made sign and two bright awnings over the front windows. A quick walk-through of our store, the Timberdoodle, will reveal candles, purses, housewares, signs, gourmet food, fair trade baskets, blouses, toys and games, and home décor. Our inventory constantly changes, and our many loyal shoppers keep returning to see our newest products. We also maintain a used book nook tucked in a niche upstairs, featuring a comfortable chair and a grand selection of reading material. Most of the Bookworm books retire here, after being passed around our entire circle. When everyone has finished a book, if the owner agrees, we "doodle it"—donate it to the Timberdoodle. The used books are priced at one-quarter of the cover price so they move fast. Who knows, these books may prevent some poor bookless traveler from going completely bonkers.

We are looking spring in the eye now, aware that Mother Nature could toss one more snowstorm our way, but nothing that will last. Tonight we are gathered at Jean's table, and the discussion is lively. Her table features a tall arrangement in the center and a repurposed bottle, slumped into a rustic rectangular shape with tapered edges, rests on each of our plates. Jean's husband finds interesting bottles in the recycling shack, then heats them in his kiln on metal trays he's fashioned to accommodate different bottle sizes. These particular slumped bottles are about the size of butter dishes and will blend with any set of dishes. Each one features an artistic rendering of his name etched on the corner. After admiring each one and complimenting his work, we stow our new bottle-dishes in our bags.

Jean serves her five-star lasagne, explaining the two versions: one with meat, one with spinach. She assures us she used separate utensils to prevent cross-contamination, and regales us with her latest book purchase tale.

Our Jean, the most frugal Bookworm in our group, stood in line and paid full price for a brand new hard back copy of *The Master Butcher's Singing Club*, by Louise Erdrich. She declares the money and time well-invested; she even had an enjoyable wait in line, chatting with other book buyers! Adventure follows Jean everywhere she goes.

Already established as one of our favorite authors, Erdrich delivered her best book thus far, a heavy tome relating the story of a soldier who marries his best friend's pregnant widow and emigrates from Germany to America, opening a butcher shop in a tiny North Dakota town. The intricate story line and complex characters keep the reader involved from the first word to the last. Erdrich excels at creating hilarious scenes; scenes leaving the reader in a helpless muddle, severely cramped from laughing madly while curled up in the reading position. One scene that springs to mind is in *Tales of Burning Love*, a story about a man who has been married and divorced four times and is allegedly dead. Somehow, Erdrich manages to place his four ex-wives together in a car, in the middle of a snowstorm, lodged in a snowdrift overnight. They each take turns clearing snow from the tail pipe to prevent suffocation, surviving on candy bars from someone's purse. These brutal circumstances motivate them to share memories of Jack, their only common thread, and his various plights and incidents.

When we all enjoy a certain book, such as *The Master Butcher's Singing Club*, we bestow our highest honor upon it, namely the Bookworms Stamp of Approval. An invisible award, the stamp is applied with gusto by the person who last read the book, as soon as we agree the book is worthy of this accolade. Striking the book with a tightly closed fist, as if with a gavel, lends a sense of finality and closure to the ritual, effectively granting highest rankings in all categories:

- interesting subject
- earned 'real' awards (i.e., National Book Award, Pulitzer, etc.)
- writing style
- realistic, memorable characters
- resolution (does it leave us hanging or provide the closure we crave?)
- punctuation (the new trend toward non-punctuation is disturbing and not well-tolerated by most of us)
- margin sizes (we need *some* white space)
- type size (we are disinclined toward small type)
- overall length

The last four categories are only important in less-well-written books; we've all read books solely because they feature wide margins and large type, and we're sometimes pleasantly surprised. Many of the fluffy sandwich books boast these formatting elements. A book with cardboard characters and a lack of punctuation is difficult to read, and not worth the time invested—by the time the fifty-page rule is observed, resentment has escalated to such a level it's impossible to read anything else, for at least five minutes.

Confession isn't over: Jean casually mentions her participation in the *other* book club in town! It is a co-ed, traditional-style book club, meeting monthly at a local restaurant. The members take turns suggesting a book, everyone buys it and reads it before the next meeting, when they thoroughly discuss and dissect the book. The author's style and the characters' motives are called into question; the word 'symbolism' is bandied about. Jean, a double agent who has successfully infiltrated the traditional readers' group, admits our book club has a superior structure and will last longer due to our freedom to choose what we read as we go along. For that matter, we aren't even limited to full-length books, as several of us have shared articles and word puzzles during our monthly meetings.

We have finished our lasagne only to be presented with Jean's berry pie for dessert. Jean and Angie are two of the best pie makers around, and we're lucky enough to have both of them in our book club. Jean makes one more announcement this evening: she's turning 70 this summer, and deems it time for her acting debut. She has the lead part in a comedic play scheduled to perform in August and she's learning her lines, which must be delivered quickly and clearly, with impeccable timing. Stage presence is one of Jean's gifts; the rich timbre of her voice carries well, making the most public of speeches seem like an intimate conversation. She was a nurse in a former life, and I'm sure her voice alone afforded many a despairing patient a measure of comfort. The stage is a wonderful place for such a voice, and Jean is using several different methods of memorization to learn her lines. Besides reading the script, she created a tape recording of the entire play, with herself reading her lines and a friend reading the other players' lines, to play while she cleans the house or goes for a walk. She shares some acting tricks with us, such as lifting her voice at the end of a sentence, almost as if she's asking a question, to communicate a Southern accent. She somehow adopts the play character without compromising her own personality, lending a new vigor to an old story.   Jean is living the phrase "Age Brilliantly", and we Bookworms aspire to do the same.

Our discussion flows to the small-town impact on 'private' clubs. We have all been accosted by those in town interested in joining Bookworms Anonymous, sometimes with a friendly inquiry, sometimes a snooty demand. One woman made a reference to our book club in the grocery store the other day, asking if we were allowing any new members to join our "precious little club." Like a mother bear, my instinct was to protect the club and prevent this condescending, romance-novel-reading woman from penetrating our circle. I explained that we host at each other's houses and we are unable to accommodate any more people at our tables. Undeterred, she suggested the library, or, if it's too difficult to be quiet, the bar! I volleyed with a suggestion to start her own club, inviting people who read the same types of books she reads. Eventually she drifted off, discouraged by the effort of individual thought. Other people have made oblique references to a 'private book club' in our presence, leaving no doubt which club they meant.

Tonight we agree to maintain our group as is, precious or not, due mainly to the perfect blending of our seven personalities and the way we fit around the table. Increasing our membership would negatively impact the book swapping: with seven members, it frequently takes eight to ten months for a given book to be read by everyone; more members would stretch circulation time longer than a year! Since we don't all read at the same pace, the pressure on slower readers would increase in a larger group, compromising the casual, comfortable atmosphere of our coterie. All of this discussion about the traditional-style reading club reinforces the friendly feeling and purpose of our septemvirate; we started meeting eight years ago, and our meetings are still dynamic, fresh and fun. I hope my daughters start their own groups some day, and experience the joy of this unique blend of good food, great friends, and books, books, books.

Besides the latest Erdrich tome, this month's selections include:

When My Sister Was Cleopatra Moon, by Frances Park

I Am Charlotte Simmons, by Tom Wolfe

Gentlemen and Players, by Joanne Harris

Nineteen Minutes, by Jodi Picoult

Lottery, by Patricia Wood

After we recover from Jean's confession and progress from dessert to decaf, Janelle presents a book she found at a consignment store for twenty-five cents: *When My Sister Was Cleopatra Moon*, by Frances Park. Now, this selection honors our frugality focus! Twenty-five cents is the least amount anyone in this group has paid for a book (not counting gifts, which are free). That alone deserves an award! This particular book is an easy read, a great sandwich book to be enjoyed between two heavier tomes. It's about two Korean-American sisters, told in both past and present tense by jumping back and forth in alternating chapters. Cleopatra is the older sister, known for her mesmerizing effect on men of all ages; her younger sister Marcy adores and idolizes her. They grow up near Washington, DC and go their separate ways as adults, Marcy to an Indian Reservation, running a secondhand store, and Cleopatra to California selling gourmet food sauces. This story is a lot like real life: mainly happy, with some great sadness sprinkled here and there.

Christine is returning a great Joanne Harris novel, *Gentlemen and Players*, but only three of us have read it so far and it's nearly impossible to review it without spoiling it for the next reader. The story takes place in Britain at a boys' day school and follows the lives of a few students and teachers. Harris tells this story like a chess game, complete with strategically positioned players, nerve-wracking suspense, and a blindsiding checkmate in the end. Upon finishing this labyrinthine tale, one is compelled to re-read it immediately in search of clues foreshadowing the outcome. This book may require a new award to properly recognize its superb craftsmanship and perfect construction.

Kayaking weather has not yet arrived, but Christine is planning ahead. This summer she has a few three- or four-day trips planned on the Great Lakes, and she's trying to reconcile her two favorite hobbies so she can enjoy them both. "I don't mind the weather, you know—I've paddled in rain, cold and damp, in heat with high humidity, in wind and high waves...I just can't stand not reading! Some trips are several days long—can you imagine seeing no words for a week?" Christine's laughing about this predicament, but the rest of us are a bit shaken by this visualization. Never considering the logistics of reading on a kayaking/camping trip, we'd all assumed she had some sort of dry bag in which to stow her books. Christine continues, "I can only read the tent pitching instructions so many times. Each time brings me closer to insanity. I've even thought about writing to the company with an idea for more interesting reading material, maybe a word game or something, printed on the inside of the tent so people won't suffer so much when they're out in the wild. The wordless wild."

"Don't you have a dry pack or some such to store books?" Angie finally asks. The rest of us nod like bobble heads, wondering the same thing.

"Well, I first tried carrying a book in my day pack, but I dropped it once right near the edge of the water. The book was fairly wet, and coated with sticky wet sand. So, the next thing I tried was a plastic zipper bag. I sealed the book in and wouldn't you know, I dropped it in knee-deep water! The zipper bag was not water tight, ladies. The book was completely drenched." We're unable to control our gasps; Christine nods in acknowledgement, in full disclosure mode now, "One time I managed to get the book to shore on a beautiful summer day and set it on a dry rock. I forgot where the book was and dropped my wet gear on it, and ruined the cover!"

"What are you going to do, girl? Stop taking books with you? There must be a way for you to keep them dry." Angie seems the most upset by this concept of bookless travel.

"I may have a solution for this coming summer, but it will be a hassle. I'm going to triple bag the books—put the book in the first bag, then put that bag in a bag, then put them in another bag. All zipper-style bags. I can't consider going without a book—I'd have a panic attack! How would I even fall asleep at night without reading?"

"You'd be lying there reading the damn tent instructions," remarks Jean gravely, "What a ghastly predicament."

"Water isn't the only trouble with reading on my kayak trips. I dried out the one book that was drenched and was reading it near the campfire last fall, and as the sun crept lower in the sky I kept nudging myself closer to the fire to illuminate my pages. Suddenly I realized I was *way* too close to the fire!"

"Was the smell of burning hair your first sign of trouble?" Janelle asks; we all laugh, picturing Christine stretched out near the fire ignoring her own safety for the sake of reading.

"Worse than that, I almost caught the book on fire! I would've had to read the damn tent wall again!" Amid the hoots of laughter, someone says we'll all pitch in and buy Christine a head lamp for reading and some kind of dry bag storage for her books. She says she never brings any Bookworms Anonymous books on her water adventures, but if she restricts herself to reading penny dreadfuls or bodice rippers while she's kayaking, she might as well go back to the directions on the tent wall.

I'm finally ready to present *Lottery* by Patricia Wood, reading the first sentence aloud to the group to set the tone and entice everyone: 'My name is Perry L. Crandall and I am not retarded'. I had read an article about this book and searched until I found it in one of Chicago's biggest book stores. It's a great story told in the first person by a borderline-retarded man in his early thirties who lives with his grandma until she dies, and is regarded as a burden and an embarrassment by his mother and siblings. When Perry wins the lottery, his formerly estranged relatives crawl from beneath their rocks to persuade him to share his millions. I found myself emotionally involved throughout this story, alternately cheering for Perry and anxiously willing him to recognize his relatives' motives. It's a quick read with great characterization and a heartwarming glimpse of relationships.

After quickly working through my stack I grant Jen the floor. I sense her low-level anxiety as she begins reviewing tentatively, looking everywhere except at Jean and Angie. She's holding up a well-worn copy of *The Handmaid's Tale* by Margaret Atwood. "I've never told you this before, but Atwood isn't my favorite author." I quickly agree; I'd only read Atwood in the past to appease Jean and Angie. While Jean shrieked in disbelief, unable to fathom a woman who doesn't identify with Atwood's feministic themes, Angie sighed with resignation, "I suspected as much."

Jen continued, "I want to say I didn't like it, but it must be a good book because I was unable to stop reading. The subject is distasteful and disturbing, but it's memorable. My husband didn't see a problem with disallowing women to work or have any money of their own. I told him about the women in the book, allowed only to be wives or housekeepers or handmaids—baby machines—reproducing at men's whim. The most unsettling aspect was the women aren't allowed to read because they might learn something. I found the whole male-dominated society rather repulsive!"

"It makes you think, though, and that's the wonderful thing about Atwood," Jean says.

"I like reading the light, fluffy books; my life is too complicated right now to handle these heavy issues and disturbing ideas. As far as feminism, I want to earn my own money and make my own decisions. And I want men to open the doors and pick up the tab, keep the vehicles operating, do all the outside maintenance, *and* bring me flowers." Jen's comments are met with laughter and agreement as we consider this perfect world she's envisioned.

"A husband has never been shot while doing the dishes," Janelle adds, "and we deserve to be treated like the princesses we are."

We continue reviewing the books we've read, each review starting quickly and gradually slowing down, adding details, pausing, waiting for someone to extend a hand and grab the book. Occasionally there's a book no one wants to take, and that's okay. We all have different tastes and one of our unspoken rules is to celebrate the variety rather than coerce each other to read what we've read. Gentle persuasion is tolerated, but pressure is implicitly prohibited.

Information-packed as it was, this meeting is a short one. Spring Fever has replaced Cabin Fever, and we're all eager to enjoy the waning evening light as we leave Jean's and lug our books outside. The fact that we're still in slush purgatory is barely noticed as we anticipate reading our fresh stacks of books.

Jean's Menu

Lasagne*

Tossed Salad

Garlic Bread

Fresh Pineapple

Berry Pie*

Coffee* Shiraz* Piesporter* Ice Water

*recipes included in Appendix C

I read until the cows came home, and I'll read until
they leave again.

Chapter Five

My sister sounded excited and a little breathless on the phone when she called to report her husband had started a new hobby: reading. She quickly listed the books he'd read (no Bookworms books yet, but *Lottery* was slated next) and shared a couple of his comments. He'd actually said reading was better than watching TV! Jen hadn't recovered from that revelation when he went so far as to deem TV unnecessary. "Cancel the satellite!" he'd sung out, "We'll just sit here and read." Jen was speechless.

This qualifies as very exciting news, since as readers we are always happy to welcome another to our society. He reads faster than Jen, blasting through four books in six days, and he teases Jenny for her slow pace. Jen's voice lowers conspiratorially as she continues, "It's so cool he reads now, because he *gets* why I like to read, and he read a whole book last weekend, but…" she drops to a whisper, "he bends the binding backwards." At my gasp, she admits quickly, still whispering, "I want to encourage his reading, so I haven't told him about the Commandments yet. At least he's not dog-earing the pages!" I tried to picture her husband reading his book enthusiastically, absorbing the words quickly, blithely bending the binding and setting the book, open, face down on the arm of his chair, eating greasy potato chips and leaving evidence on every page…my thoughts were spinning out of control! It was overwhelming. I took a couple cleansing breaths and thought about the Commandments.

Where and when did I learn the Book Handling Commandments?   The Commandments are so ingrained, I believe they're part of my genetic makeup or basic instinct to treat books with respect and care. I would no more dog-ear a page than amputate my own foot! One would assume I was raised during the Depression, judging by the way I anxiously conserve and preserve everything. This tendency extends beyond books: clothes are folded before they're placed in the hamper, uneaten crackers fastidiously rewrapped and zip-locked, book bindings never bent backwards, pages always pristine. A scrawled "Kellis" in light pencil is often the only indication I've ever touched a book.   So, to initiate new readers, the unsuspecting members of our bibliophilic society, I will list the Book Handling Commandments here. The following list should not be considered all-inclusive—it is impossible to predict every situation a reader might encounter. Common sense and an honest intention to preserve the book in question exactly as it was when borrowed should always be kept foremost in mind.

BOOK HANDLING COMMANDMENTS

1. Do not dog-ear pages. Always use a bookmark or memorize the page number.
2. Bookmarks must be flat so they don't strain the binding. Index cards work well, as do flat ribbons, 'regular' bookmarks found in book stores, dollar bills, and small corners torn from magazines. Thick or odd-shaped bookmarks shall not be used.
3. Do not bend the binding backward. This results in a cracked binding and greatly diminishes book life.
4. Protect books from the elements when outside—tuck inside jacket or tote bag to prevent rain, snow, and any other liquid from leaving water marks.
5. Do not read in hazardous conditions, for example, while bathing or bicycling, eating spaghetti or kayaking. Magazines were created for these applications.
6. Carry a book at all times when leaving the house, and always treat books with respect. A book represents someone's ideas, determination and perseverance and deserves, at the very least, respectful handling.
7. It's okay to inhale the scent of the pages. Especially *new* pages. In fact, I recommend it.
8. Do not write in books, except to note the owner's name. If a particular passage in a book demands notation, use a Post-It note or copy it down in a planner. An exception to this rule is text books, self-help books, diaries, and other types of education books, wherein it is acceptable to highlight and/or write small notes in the margins.
9. When a hardback book has a dust jacket, the jacket must be removed while reading. It's important to remember that a dust jacket is *not* a bookmark. It was created to keep

dust off the book while shelved. Store the dust jacket in a safe place, such as resting atop the books on the bookcase, until finishing the book.

10. When eating or drinking while reading, keep the book out of the path of food and liquid by holding the book near the middle of the table, on the far side of the plate.

11. It is allowed, and encouraged, to read while performing certain mindless tasks that won't be compromised by holding a book, such as rocking a baby, waiting on hold, or during the commercials that interrupt a favorite show.

12. None of these rules apply to magazines, which contain time-sensitive material best enjoyed while still fresh, and aren't intended to last as long as books. Magazines are like Black Velvet, to be chugged without tasting, while books are like Crown Royal, to be sipped and savored and shared with friends.

Breaking one of the above Commandments incurs serious penalties, including the release of negative energy into the Universe, loss of sleep (as anxiety over the crime against literacy mentally replays every night), bad book karma, and possibly even loss of book borrowing privileges. Those who break a Commandment find the penalties so severe and humiliating they generally don't mention them to other readers. Sometimes the treatment of the offender is subtle and difficult to notice. Requests to borrow books may be met with a change of subject or a suggestion to get a library card; oblique comments regarding the condition of a previously borrowed book, returned dog-eared and watermarked, may be whispered until the broken record of the transgression plays over and over and over, driving one insane. It's possible to damage a book by mistake, of course. A book can slip from under a jacket and land in a puddle; the pocket it's in can come unbuttoned, inviting snow and rain onto the pages; it can just slip from one's hand as a result of carrying too many things at one time. The best response to these situations is to adopt an aggressive offense and explain the problem to the owner before she asks.

If the unthinkable happens and a borrowed book is damaged despite the best, most sincere efforts to maintain its integrity, there is really only one thing to do: replace the book. Tie it with a pretty ribbon and present it with flair to the owner.

There are remedial actions for slightly damaged books. A warm iron can restore a wet page to near perfection if applied before the page puckers; tape and/or lamination can repair and preserve a small tear in the cover or one of the pages. A replacement cover can be downloaded from the Internet, printed on card stock, laminated, and applied to the book with archival tape. My sister once bought a used book on the Internet and discovered the last 20 pages were missing! Forced to buy another copy to discover the ending, she photocopied the last 20 pages from her replacement book, trimmed them to fit, and inserted them in the first copy she'd purchased. Now she had one to keep and one to loan out.

We're meeting at Angie's tonight, and now that winter has finally bowed out, I'm full of energy. I decide to bicycle the five miles to her house carrying my books on my back. My legs are rubbery and unreliable when I arrive, but I feel joyous and energized. The air is sweet with lilacs—our prolific lilac trees perfume the entire town in early summer making it impossible to be anything but happy—and the lake looks fresh and fabulous from Angie's dining room windows.

My first personal encounter with Angie was also my first day of ninth grade. The first day of the school year is always a half-day with each class only lasting a few minutes, more of an orientation than a regular school day, and there isn't much time to learn a routine or get acquainted with teachers. I already knew who Angie was, of course, since she lived a mile and a half away at the other end of town, but I had never really talked to her and didn't know what to expect. English was my favorite subject and Angie had earned a reputation as a tough but fair teacher; taking her class was both exciting and daunting. Once we were all seated, she distributed a detailed syllabus. This was the first time I'd encountered a syllabus, and hers represented an impressive level of organization. At the end of class, she asked me to stay behind for a moment. I will never forget our conversation.

Angie got right to the point. "We need to get one thing straight. You and I have to get along for four years and I don't tolerate any funny business in my class." It took a moment for my brain to decode what my ears were hearing…what had I done wrong in the first eleven minutes?

"I'm looking forward to your class, and I like your syllabus," I said lamely, my confrontation avoidance anxiety kicking into high gear.

"I just want to make sure you realize I demand a lot of my students and I know you can deliver. I have high expectations for you and I will do my best to help you meet them." I just nodded at this, and she excused me from the room. Although this felt like a rocky start, we quickly found a successful relationship style. She even let me read my book in class during the grammar lessons after I passed all of her pre-tests! Her reputation for being tough and fair was well-earned; she taught us so well I applied most of her lessons on organization, note-taking and essay writing to my other classes. She was easily the best teacher I've had, in high school and college. Her syllabus proved to be accurate down to the day, as well, making her the only person I know able to predict and control reality.

Now, we are fellow Bookworms, business partners and part-owners of the Timberdoodle, and she is one of my favorite people. When we arrive at her house for the Bookworms meeting tonight, her organizational skills are evident: her table is set for seven with a vase full of lilacs in the center, four different types of salad, each with its own dressing, and two bottles of wine. Each place setting is flanked with silverware and a cloth napkin, and a glass of ice water with a lemon wedge. Everyone arrives quickly and settles around her table, complimenting her beautiful salads and fresh flowers.

Tonight's meeting is pure joy, an effortless gathering to celebrate reading, summer's imminence, and our overdue emergence from dark houses. After such a lengthy winter, we're glad to greet the sun! Angie's salads are a hit; they taste like summer, and although it's still cool outside, we're ready to forgo hot, hearty meals for a few months. Jen brings news of her new baby, revealing his name to everyone: Tucker Andrew. Her many months of hand-wringing, obsessive contemplation, her heart-wrenching self-doubt and careful consideration, finally resulted in a name rhyming with pucker and sucker. Jen explains, "I know people might call him 'Tucker the f—er', but we figured kids will call each other names anyway, so we might as well make it easy for them." This comment is met with hoots of laughter and agreement from around the table.

The meal passes quickly due to everyone's heightened energy, and we move on to the book reviews, which include the following:

Code Talker, by Joseph Bruchac
Bridge of Sighs, by Richard Russo
The Last Lecture, by Randy Pausch
The Last Chinese Chef, by Nicole Mones
Sister Mine, by Tawni O'Dell

Janelle is chosen to start things out because she is the most prepared, with notes jotted about some of the books she brought. She starts with *Code Talker*, written at a young adult level, making it a fast read. It explores the role Native Americans played in WWII communicating over the air in Navajo language. The Japanese never cracked the code and the entire operation remained classified information, thereby cheating the Navajo Indians out of proper recognition for their efforts until fifty years after the war ended. While there is mention of some cruel acts perpetrated by both the Americans and the Japanese, this portion of the truth is heavily veiled to appeal to the intended young adult audience. *Code Talker* is a great story about unsung heroes.

The Last Chinese Chef is Janelle's next presentation. A somewhat predictable but highly enjoyable tale, it's about a recently widowed woman who travels to China to address a paternity suit concerning her husband. She writes articles for a food magazine, and interviews a contestant in a prestigious Chinese culinary contest as professional justification for her trip. The book features excerpted writings from the 'real' Last Chinese Chef, the grandfather of the contestant/love interest she is interviewing. The complexities and symbolism of Chinese food, from preparation to presentation to enjoyment, are explained and celebrated; a few of the recipes are included at the end of the book.

After Janelle presents a few other books she's read, it's Jen's turn to sift through her stack and share some books with us. Jen first presents *Bridge of Sighs*, the newest book by one of her favorite authors. The Bookworms first encountered Richard Russo when I found the book *Empire Falls*, a great story about a diner in small-town Vermont, owned and managed by a recently divorced man whose ex-wife lives across town with her muscle-bound boyfriend. The book explores small-town life and relationships, and it hooked every one of us on Richard Russo. We've read everything he's written and while some are better than others, we find relatable characters in all of his books. The *Bridge of Sighs* is beyond Russo's typical story, taking place in the US and Italy, spanning the lifetime of a group of friends and their families. His typical small-town setting is here, but it's balanced by international moves, celebrity status (one of the friends becomes a renowned artist), and the melancholy, complex characters he's known for. I don't want to say too much about this book; it's heavy, providing the reader with a work out while reading it, but it's difficult to put down so the work out will be a short one.

The comment about working out with a heavy book causes someone to mention reading outdoors, unofficially considered a sport in the world of literary athletics, now possible since the mercury has risen to a tolerable level.

Christine is sitting next to Jen, so she starts reviewing her stack of books next. Since she doesn't have any new books to introduce, her reviews are shorter as she just reminds us what each book is about. Most of us already know which ones we're waiting to read; Christine just hands the books off as she finishes talking about them. One of her return books, *The Magician's Assistant*, prompts a re-discussion because it's a great read in spite of its strange story line. The main character is a woman who works as a magician's assistant and marries him, despite his being gay and mourning his lover's demise. The story begins after the magician dies, and his wife/assistant Sabine discovers his Nebraska roots and a life she never imagined he had. Memories fill in the blanks throughout the book, providing the reader a complete picture of the characters' lives and explaining most of the missing details. The language used to tell this story is magical itself and we reach a consensus regarding Ann Patchett's talent for telling tales. If she wrote an instruction manual on how to change a tire or cook an egg, it would be a fascinating read.

Christine tells us about her summer plans: a kayak camping trip near Pictured Rocks on Lake Superior, and a paddle across the Straits of Mackinac. She keeps her kayak on her car most of the summer, ready for a spontaneous paddle at any opportunity.

I brought *Sister Mine* tonight, a new book by Tawni O'Dell. Since we enjoyed one of her previous novels, I picked up this new one and read the first sentence in the store. I was hooked right away—the main character is a forty-year-old retired policewoman and single mother who has moved home to the hills of Pennsylvania to open a taxi cab business and stay close to her son, the 24-year-old town deputy. Shae-Lynn wears outrageous outfits, talks like a trucker and throws men out of bars, creating several hilarious situations to keep the reader alert and interested. She has a deceased father who still figures prominently in her life, close coal-miner friends who nearly died in a recent mining accident and are seeking reward or revenge for substandard working conditions, and a previously presumed-dead sister who shows up and involves Shae-Lynn in her morally appalling lifestyle.

We progress around the table, listening to book reviews and grabbing those we want to read next, bartering with each other when necessary, promising to read certain books first and return them at the next meeting. We finish a little earlier than usual, still full of spring energy, and I realize a little late how heavy my new pile of books is strapped on my back.

I decide to ride my bike through town and take an alternate route home to breathe in the lilacs and savor their brief appearance. The main street is festooned with flags, lending our town an air of dignity and pride. My ride home is uneventful, with only one vehicle on the road, the sun illuminating the fresh leaves on the hardwoods along the way. The meeting replays in my mind and I think about my new nephew, picturing him growing up and finding trouble like little boys do. His eyes already have a playful sparkle and he is directly descended from two known smartasses. I envision him as a boy of three or four, eyes glittering with mischief, extending his hand for a handshake as he's been taught and announcing proudly, "Pleased to meet you. My name is Tucker the f—er!" before racing off to hide behind his mother. I laugh to myself and glance around to make sure there are no witnesses (there aren't any). When I arrive home, my legs are nearly non-functional from the ride; I collapse on the front porch and start reading.

Angie's Menu

Enlightened Waldorf Salad*

Bean & Onion Salad*

Pasta Shrimp Salad

Cauliflower, Carrot, Pepper Salad*

Biscotti*

Coffee* Merlot* Riesling* Ice Water

*recipes included in Appendix C

Preliminary interviews for Bookworms Anonymous

Chapter Six

Every now and then, even with the superior recommendations of the Bookworms, I encounter a book I don't like. The books I choose usually grab me in the first sentence or paragraph, but occasionally a book is difficult to appreciate, requiring more time and effort to fully experience. Such a book is the reason the Fifty Page Test was invented. Angie established this rule when her students complained about reading one of her selections; she allowed them to choose another, but only after reading the first fifty pages to give the book a fair chance. Usually, if a reader is fifty pages into a book, she knows whether or not she wants to continue. It's a chance to determine the level of commitment to the book. When I read a book that flunks the Fifty Page Test, I note 'stinkeroo', or merely '≠50', in my book journal reminding me to warn others. Bookworm members sometimes bring books they didn't enjoy to the meeting in case one of us would like to read them, and/or to warn us away. Sometimes, a book flunks the Fifty Page Test solely because of the weather.

Summer has finally arrived in the UP, meaning we can expect three random, perfect days of weather. Yes, for three non-contiguous days, there are no mosquitoes, humidity, rain or wind; people flock to the beaches, parking their cars on both sides of the highway at the ones with the best sand, where the locals hang out. These days of perfection are impossible to accurately predict; the weatherman has a well-earned reputation for inaccurate forecasts no matter the season, forcing us to act as amateur meteorologists by glancing outside, observing the weather, and reacting accordingly. A perfect summer day, rare as it is, demands priority. It demands notice and commitment. It demands, if it's a work day, calling in sick. It's impossible to resist: a light breeze, warm lake water, hot sun, no mosquitoes or biting flies. *This* is the reason we live here. Three flawless, elusive, effervescent summer days provided by fickle Mother Nature as a reward for surviving winter. Definitely difficult to focus on a book, even the best book, on such a day.

At the beach today, I run into a couple of friends I haven't seen lately. As old friends do, we take up as if we just saw each other yesterday, erasing the three-year hiatus. When they mention their recent Yooper anniversary card exchange, I look puzzled, so he starts:

"We went out to dinner in the Sault for our anniversary. On the way there, she says 'I didn't even get you a card!' Of course,

I didn't have a card for her either so it didn't matter, but she said that wouldn't do."

At his pause, his wife continues the story, "So he says 'I've got an idea. I'll explain to you when we get there.' So I'm thinking he's expecting me to forget all about it, but no, he takes me to Wal-Mart and we go straight to the card section. He says 'find the card you would have bought me, and I'll find the one I'd buy for you.' We exchanged the cards we chose, read them, put them back on the rack, and left the store!"

"Cheapest card I ever got!" The husband is laughing hysterically by now, slapping his leg for effect. "I should call Jeff Foxworthy with that story! It's almost as good as when we moved the entire living room out to Main Street and served daiquiris to people going by!" His wife just rolls her eyes and grins.

We pass the afternoon on the beach, telling stories and watching the kids in the water. My book is stashed in my tote bag, of course, but I'm reluctant to pull it out and miss this day. I'll read tomorrow, to divert myself from the humidity and mosquitoes that will have returned by then.

∾

The day of the meeting arrives, ushered in by humidity and attended by the ubiquitous mosquitoes. We're gathering at Janelle's this time; her husband and sons are kayaking and building a bonfire on the beach, and she has spent the day preparing, cleaning and rearranging her porch to accommodate us around her large glass table. Her porch features a grand view of the resort she and her husband purchased, situated on the shore for optimal freighter viewing, and she has clear vinyl panels installed to help block the wind and fool the mosquitoes. She is serving Asian fare this evening, starting with slaw salad and homemade ginger dressing, then spring rolls, neat packets lined up on a platter as in a magazine photo, and ending with chocolate cake. As we start eating, someone asks about the spring rolls—they look perfect, professionally wrapped and tucked, and brimming with matchstick-chopped vegetables. Janelle grabs a rice wrap, which looks like a small, thin disc, and explains how to use it, "It's easy to do, just soak the rice wrap in water for a few minutes, then use it like a tortilla and wrap it around your choice of filling. I found them in the Asian market in Lansing. They keep forever while they're dry, so you can stock up and store them in the cupboard." We pass the rice wrap around the table, commenting on Janelle's cleverness and culinary creativity.

When it's time for dessert, Janelle produces a perfect chocolate cake, a round, single-layer fudge-like confection cut into wedges and served with Cool Whip and fresh berries. We rave about the cake, moist and decadent, and she shares the recipe with us: one cake mix and ten ounces of diet soda! It's hard to believe, but we were eating a regular chocolate cake mix, combined with a diet Faygo Crème Soda. Delectable. Her sons make a brief appearance after dessert upon their return home, greeting us like two gentlemen in training and displaying identical toothy grins before disappearing into the house.

The stacks of books are shorter than usual this evening, as the weather impacted everyone's reading time and habits. We're all in summer mode now, relaxed and warm, cheerful and carefree, footloose in our sleeveless shirts and sandals rather than bundling up and donning boots and scarves. Summer affords such freedom from winter's bulky layers! When Angie asks about a book in Jean's stack, Jean begins reviewing and we progress around the table from there.

Tonight's books include:

Sight Hound, by Pam Houston

Lost & Found, by Carolyn Parkhurst
The Monsters of Templeton, by Lauren Groff
The Story of Edgar Sawtelle, by David Wroblewski
It Takes a Village Idiot, by Jim Mullen

Jean starts with *It Takes a Village Idiot*, a fun story about a guy living in New York City who just purchased a farm in upstate New York. He and his wife are unfamiliar with rural life, and the reader laughs out loud at his revelations about unsolicited neighborly assistance, community events, and honesty between strangers. This book eventually made a complete circle, borrowed and read by each of us, and earned the Bookworms Stamp of Approval on its entertainment merit alone.

Before the meeting, my day was hectic, causing me to skip my routine preparation. I usually think about each book for a moment, silently preparing to present them to the group, but today I gathered my books on my way out the door. At the meeting when everyone started reviewing their books, I just listened and enjoyed their presentations. Suddenly it was my turn, and my lack of attention to the books I'd brought developed into a crisis, resulting in lame reviews.

"Let's see," Suffering from sudden onset memory lapse, I desperately skim the back of the book for a clue about the story line, "oh yea, this book reminds me of that one book we read with the animals' points of view. Or maybe it reminded me more of the one in Alaska with the mother-in-law." Immediately, everyone tries to trigger my newly feeble memory.

"The one by Haddon? The autistic story?"

"…No…" My recollection of the book in my hand is fading from dark gray to black.

"Is it the one with the mother-in-law and the son, who is the husband, dies, and the girl, the wife, moves in, from Alaska to California, and their place looked like the Salvation Army or something?"

"...No..." Now I'm recalling *those* books, and still can't remember the one I'm holding! Finally, a character from the book starts to emerge from the mental gloom. "Ok, I've got it. It's all coming back to me now. The main character is a woman named...um...well, it doesn't matter what her name is, but she always needs someone to take care of her and all of the other characters in the book, including her pets and their veterinarian, worry about this woman and act like she's going to fall apart any minute." There are no takers, so I continue, "oh yes, and the dog, Dante, has a main voice. He's missing a leg...or maybe two...and the vet tried a prosthetic leg but it only worked temporarily." I'm holding the book up now to show everyone the cover, the title *Sight Hound* clearly displayed above Pam Houston's name.

Jen challenges me, adopting an accusatory squint, "Did you *really* read this book?"

"Yes I did, I remember carrying it around. I remember turning the pages. The chapters told from the pets' points of view are good. I just don't care too much about the main character. She needs to pull up her socks and get on with it." Janelle takes the book, interested in reading the animals' points of view, but unsure about the prosthetic dog leg experiment.

My next book is *Lost and Found* by Carolyn Parkhurst. I'd read this one more recently than *Sight Hound*, lending my review more confidence. "This was a fun read, about a mother and daughter in a reality TV show," groans are heard from around the table, "No, it's not that bad, it's a TV show on the order of The Amazing Race, with teams of two people, but they also have to locate specific objects." The Worms are really groaning now, talking about wasting time watching drivel and reality television being anything but real, most of them never having heard of

The Amazing Race, let alone watched it. When the cacophony subsides, I resume, "Each couple has a secret the producers hope they'll reveal on tape. One couple is an 'ex-gay' couple, now in a straight marriage and constantly spouting religious platitudes; one is a former child star who is trying to put her face back in the spotlight; and the two main characters are mother and daughter." Now I'm hearing phrases like "oh, a mother-daughter story might be alright" and "we haven't read a mother-daughter in a while".

I continue again, "The daughter had a baby recently, and no one knew she was pregnant." The other Bookworms are gasping, wondering aloud how on earth a child still living at home could carry a baby to term without anyone noticing.

"It sounds like a soap opera combined with a game show," Jen remarks.

"That's too farfetched; I don't know if I can suspend my disbelief that far," says Christine, and the others seem to agree.

Desperate, I add random details to entice someone to read the book. "Each chapter has a different narrator! Some of their life stories and circumstances are interesting!" Finally, I pull out the stock phrase we all use, which rarely causes a fellow Bookworm to read a book, but makes us feel better as we utter it: "I'm glad I read it!" Everyone points toward the ceiling and sings out at once: "Doodle it!"

Carolyn Parkhurst's other book, *The Dogs of Babel*, was a popular Bookworm book and still resides on my bookshelf. I'm not sure why *Babel* attracted me, unless it was the lesson contained therein: to understand someone, one must learn their language. In the beginning of the story, the reader meets Paul, a widower who doesn't accept his wife's recent death and wonders if it was the accident it appeared, or a planned suicide. She fell from a tree in their back yard, dying instantly, and the only witness was the family dog. A Rhodesian Ridgeback, Lorelei is an extremely smart dog, but she can't speak English. Paul, a linguistics professor at the local college, is convinced that Lorelei wants to tell him what happened to his wife; he takes a sabbatical and dedicates himself to teaching Lorelei various methods of communication. In one particularly disturbing part of the book, he even considers jaw-altering surgery to modify the shape of Lorelei's face to help her verbalize words (he stops before Lorelei is harmed). In the end, the reader learns what happened to Paul's wife when Paul finally relaxes and Lorelei relates the events in her own way. Some of the Bookworms thought Paul's actions were completely irrational and unbelievable, but I think he is a romantic figure experiencing profound grief, unable to accept the unthinkable, handling it the only way he can.

We have one more book tonight about dogs: the highly acclaimed tome that garnered Oprah's attention moments after the ink dried on the pages. David Wroblewski's *The Story of Edgar Sawtelle*. This book has been discussed, dissected, scrutinized and dismembered, so I won't review it here except to say it's worth reading and deserving of shelf space, and everyone in our group agrees it was a great story in spite of its loose, somewhat disappointing ending. The research on dog breeding by character trait especially interested me; the volume of data in the meticulous files maintained by the Sawtelle family for generations, including custom-made charts and detailed lineage information, really drew me in. The author is holding an ongoing conversation about his book and its characters, easily found on the Internet for those curious about his intentions, methods, or future plans.

Janelle has a couple of stories for us. First, she presents Jean with a replacement copy of *The Robber Bride* by Margaret Atwood, complete with a pretty blue and green ribbon tied around it, explaining, "I broke the rules and tried reading this book in the hot tub, and it slipped from my fingers! I dried it out, but it's all bloated now so I just bought you a new one."

"Oh, wonderful! I can't believe you bought a new book. I found that one at the thrift store, girl." Jean is grinning and chuckling, untying the ribbon. "I really didn't need it to be replaced. I wasn't planning to keep it, but now that it's brand new again, I can give it as a gift to my sister! Wonderful!"

"I almost called and asked how important that book was to you, but then I decided to send the bloated copy to my sister-in-law. She's rough on her books, so she'll enjoy this one because she won't feel guilty about it ending up in worse shape than it was when she received it," Janelle explains.

"Is she the one who walked the Appalachian Trail and tore up her book?" I ask.

"Yep, she was walking along with five or six others and one of them was reading *The World According to Garp*. They started reading aloud, but it was too hard for everyone to hear, so they started passing the book back and forth between all of them. That method wasn't much fun, so someone suggested tearing out a few pages at a time and passing them from hiker to hiker. The last one to read the pages kept them for the evening campfire." Now, *there's* a situation that justifies breaking every Book Handling Commandment. Janelle continues, "At first, I thought it was disturbing to destroy a John Irving book so violently, but since so many people enjoyed it, I guess it was justified. And using the shredded pages for kindling increased the utility of the book. Someone should write to John Irving to tell him how useful his book was, both as entertainment and as heat." We laugh lightly, all of us thankful we can read inside on comfortable chairs. The act of reading mutates from a quiet, solitary pursuit to a lively participation sport when combined with hiking. The Appalachian walkers won't soon forget Irving's influence on their journey.

Janelle is presenting a book almost as long as the *Edgar Sawtelle* saga: *The Monsters of Templeton*, by Lauren Groff, a hardback boasting an enticing cover. It's an artistic rendering of a family tree, black on a white background; some of the branches curl around tiny scenes, showcasing silhouettes of various ancestors. Planting her elbow on the table, she displays the book in one hand and begins, "It takes place in upstate New York, in a town called Templeton, which is actually Cooperstown, as it explains right in the beginning before the story starts. One of the first scenes in the story is a real crack-up...a girl in her twenties is returning home, pregnant by the professor assisting her with her doctorate, and her mother doesn't think she's real. She's this hippie dippie mother who did all sorts of questionable things back in the day, so when the girl appears in the doorway, the mother looks up from her nap and says 'stupid flashbacks' and starts rubbing her eyes, trying to make sense of what she's seeing." The Bookworms respond with various comments about hippies and flashbacks, teen pregnancy and small towns.

My mom asks, "What are the monsters in the title?"

"Well, the monsters are two things. There is a monster in the lake in town, sort of like the Loch Ness monster, but that's really a minor part of the story. The other monsters are in the girl's family tree. She starts researching her family tree when her mother finally admits she does know who her father is, after having told her for years that he was one of a few possibilities in a hippie commune; and he not only lives in town, he's related in some shirttail fashion to the hippie dippie mother." She shows us the family trees throughout the book, and a few of the photos of the ancestors featured at the beginning of the chapters. It looks like a fun story and ancient family photos always interest me; I grab the book to read it next. I finished it in the first few days following the meeting and found it complicated and compelling, but the ever-present spectre lingering in the house detracted from the overall flow of the story. My favorite sections of the book were the chapters narrated in a collective first person style by the Running Buds, a group of men who have been jogging through town on a specific route every morning, no matter the weather, for the past few decades, gossiping, sharing their lives, watching their town wake up. I could read an entire book from their point of view.

The coffee is cooling and the wine bottles are empty; the mosquitoes are arriving to adjourn our meeting. We schedule for next month fully aware we're witnessing the decline of summer. Angie wedges books in her bike basket and pedals away as my mom starts walking and the rest of us climb into our trucks, windows lowered despite the mosquitoes.

Janelle's Menu

Asian Slaw*

Spring Rolls*

Chocolate Cake*

Coffee * Shiraz * Chardonnay * Ice Water

*recipes included in Appendix C

It's a wonderful afternoon for reading, but first we must eat our lunch.

Chapter Seven

It's impossible to ignore words passing before my eyes; billboards, store signs, bumper stickers, license plates (I can usually form a word by just adding a couple letters), cereal boxes... everything contains words and I read them all. The checkout line at the store presents an especially distracting display of magazines, candy, impulse items, and sale signs. I'm quite sure I'll die reading, hopefully as an ancient lady snug in bed with a good book.

When we're driving, my husband sees entirely different signs containing no words at all. Our conversations go something like this:

"I can't believe they added an apostrophe to 'sales' on their sign! Don't people learn punctuation anymore?"

"What sign?"

"The sign back there announcing an end of year sale. It's bright pink and stuck on a power pole. You didn't see it?"

"No, I was busy looking at the deer trail crossing the road."

"Deer trail? I didn't see a deer trail."

"That's because there was no street sign."

See, we each read our own signs. Together, we can navigate just about any terrain.

When we leave town, for any reason, we usually go shopping. Living at the end of the earth necessitates stocking up on supplies whenever possible; if there's an occasion to leave the county, such as doctor appointments, dentist appointments, or visiting friends, we add stores to our itinerary to make it worth the trip.

On a recent trip downstate to visit friends, we spent part of a day at the mall. My eyes hungrily scanned every surface, reading the sales flyers, banners, and product promotions offered in every store. My daughter needed new shirts, and as our routine went, she shopped alone then called me to pay once she found them. She was in a designer clothing store, one I'd never entered, and she said she'd meet me at the entrance. I was immediately assaulted by excruciatingly loud music and pungent, perfume-scented air. This sensory overload was balanced by the dark furniture and low-light fixtures in small, cave-like niches, rendering me nearly blind. I fought the vertiginous disorientation and squinted into the gloom to locate my daughter inspecting some T-shirts, and waved to get her attention. The light was too dim for her to see me, and the music precluded normal communication as evidenced by my increasing headache, forcing me to yell, "LET'S GO!", suddenly desperate to escape. My daughter casually held up a finger to indicate she needed another moment; I tapped my wrist and jerked my head toward the cashier. We finally approached the counter, where the bubble-gum-chewing twelve-year-old cheerleader rang up our purchase and hollered, "THAT'LL BE FORTY-SIX DOLLARS AND THIRTY SEVEN CENTS, PLEASE!" I was in shock! She must have charged us double! These were two extremely thin cotton T-shirts, emblazoned with the store's name, each an unidentifiable color in the strange light. "ARE YOU SERIOUS? FORTY-SIX DOLLARS FOR TWO T-SHIRTS?" I felt monstrous screeching at this child behind the counter, but she didn't seem to notice. My mortified daughter yelled at a slightly lower volume *"Mom! Just pay! Please!"* The cashier shrieked, "WOULD YOU LIKE SOME FREE PERFUME?" I'd had enough; my head was pounding, my eyes streaming from the offensive odor, and I was sickened by the posters of scantily-clad teens emerging from the shadows. "YOU'RE DAMN RIGHT I WANT FREE PERFUME WITH TWO T-SHIRTS FOR FORTY-SIX DOLLARS!" I bellowed at the poor girl. I shoved my credit card at her and signed on the line without even checking the amount. My daughter left the store slightly richer, sporting a trendy shopping bag containing two teeny-tiny T-shirts and a free drop of perfume. What a bargain. My headache receded and my hearing returned just in time to hear my daughter accuse me of being old. "It's not a sign of age," I explained, "It's wisdom. And sensibility."

My daughter was recently sentenced to two years of orthodontia. Planning to turn this ordeal into an adventure and incorporating fun in the form of shopping into each appointment day, we selected the orthodontist based on his proximity to our favorite bookstore. We joined the frequent buyers' club and established a routine to include a visit to the bookstore and one of the cute little cafés located near the orthodontist's office. The bookstore is a two-story sanctuary, filled with all things biblio. I'd move in if they'd let me, curl up on one of their loveseats and read everything within reach. The staff is well-read and attentive without being meddlesome, always appearing at the right moment, retreating immediately if their help isn't needed. If it weren't for the orthodontist appointments, we would both fully enjoy our monthly sojourns. In fact, I will miss our little trips. Maybe I'll invent a reason to continue going...

Autumn has arrived, triggering the annual urge to shop in office supply stores. Notebooks, pens, papers, files, organizational tools and even index cards in all colors beckon me, taunting me with their implicit promises of productivity, their guarantees of satisfaction. Since it takes incredible willpower to drive past an office supply store in the fall of the year, I park in the front row and walk in confidently. I cruise the aisles, considering new calculators, the latest accounting software, new digital cameras and printers. Methodically working the store in a grid pattern, I drool on the reams of heavyweight paper, the file folders (new colors this season!), wall calendars, day planners, and fancy pens. If only I had a new office to fill with supplies! The office furniture rounds out my tour as I envision my office, twice as large as reality, mentally placing and rearranging various pieces until I'm left with a design to maximize efficiency and organization. As a reward for resisting a major purchase, I treat myself to a pack of black fine-point pens so smooth they almost write for me, and a pack of Post-It notes in trendy colors. I leave the store fulfilled, my office-supply addiction satisfied for another year.

Autumn in the UP is the best season of the year, sporting beautiful leaves along the roads and bordering the fields on the way to the meeting at Christine's. She lives in a two-story octagonal house she designed and built herself, trading and bartering with the neighbors for the more difficult portions of the project. The result is a unique abode, featuring a stone fireplace, open beams, and lots of windows, the rooms on the first floor flowing one to the next around the central vertical support column. Interesting artwork and knick knacks decorate the walls, and the open staircase rises above a built-in bookcase full of shelf-worthy reads.

As we arrive at Christine's, she directs us to her garden so we can witness her autumn squash in its glory. We follow a short path from her yard to the garden, around the large maple with the rope swing and into the field, avian hosts twittering and singing as we traipse beneath their nests. We ooh and aah over her garden, featuring an interesting boxy design and plenty of vegetables yet to harvest. She leads us back along the path to her new herb garden closer to the house for easy kitchen prep, planted in a wheel shape complete with wood spokes wide enough to access the herbs in each section. The geometry of Christine's gardens satisfies my aesthetic values; an ideal marriage of character and purpose.

It's a beautiful evening, dry and warm, and we're reluctant to end our outside tour. The food is beckoning, so we finally go in and settle around the table, already set with a large bowl of butternut squash soup at each place. A vase of wildflowers resides in the center of the table alongside a bowl of cabbage and apple salad. Two tall tapers in cut crystal candlesticks flank the flowers, the small flames lending a cozy air to our gathering. Conversation centers around winter preparation; it's time to stop acting like grasshoppers and adopt ant mode so we're not caught off-guard by an early storm. Christine has eighteen cords of wood stacked in her lean-to, ready to chuck into the woodstove when the mercury drops. Her newly purchased snow plow and pick-up truck stand ready to rearrange snow, her old tractor retired from winter duty. The first section of her driveway is several hundred feet long, and the second section even longer, but shared with a neighbor who takes turns removing snow. Plowing with a pick-up truck in a heated, enclosed cab is a huge improvement over plowing on an open tractor, and that with a recalcitrant starter!

Giddy with anxiety at the thought of autumn ending, we change the topic while we eat dessert: blueberry pound cake filled with fresh blueberries Christine picked on her recent trek along part of the North Country Hiking Trail, a 4600 mile-long trail extending from North Dakota to Pennsylvania. She backpacked along part of the section stretching across the Upper Peninsula with a group of women, primitive camping every night.

Tonight's stacks include:

The Last American Male, by Elizabeth Gilbert
Ella Minnow Pea, by Mark Dunn
The Opposite of Fate, by Amy Tan
The Hour I First Believed, by Wally Lamb
Truck: A Love Story, by Michael Perry
One True Thing, by Anna Quindlen

Everyone has a mid-sized pile of books this evening, and the cover of my top book catches someone's attention. It's a non-fiction book with a close-up photo of a man's face on the cover; an in-depth character study and biography, written by Elizabeth Gilbert (*Eat, Pray, Love*), called *The Last American Male*. Gilbert writes as a friend of the main character, yet spares no details as she illuminates both positive and negative facets of Eustace Conway's life and personality. Eustace lives in the Appalachian Mountains at a nature preserve he established to promote his life goal of living purely by his own hands. He grows or shoots all of his food, built his own house and outbuildings, generates his own electricity, and occasionally leaves his preserve to educate others how to reduce their carbon footprint. Eustace holds a few records for physical feats—he hiked the entire Appalachian Trail, traveled on horseback across the United States at breakneck speed, stopping only to sleep for four hours each night, and purchased several thousand acres of land on which he established Turtle Island Preserve. Gilbert's integrity prevents her from ignoring the negative aspects of Conway's personality, including alcohol dependence and an abusive relationship with his father, leaving the reader with a comprehensive picture of an intense, complex, highly-driven individual. Christine will read the book next because she shares many of Conway's interests. And his cover photo is cute.

Janelle is next, reviewing Wally Lamb's *The Hour I First Believed*. We all read his first two novels and we're expecting great things from this newest volume. Janelle gives it five stars and predicts it will earn the Bookworms Stamp of Approval, but remains vague about the story itself. "Don't be put off by this, but it does contain the shooting at Columbine. That isn't the whole story, and it doesn't have grisly details or anything, but the main character and his wife are both employees of the school during the shooting. Besides Columbine, it's about family history, marriage, psychology, growing up, life struggles, and it takes place in Colorado and in the northeast someplace. Maine, I think. It's large, but difficult to put down; definitely a great book." We're all reaching out by this point; she picks someone who hasn't taken any books yet this evening and gives it to her.

Janelle also brought *Ella Minnow Pea*, a great little book set on a fictional island off South Carolina, founded by the man who wrote the famous sentence using every letter of the alphabet: The quick brown fox jumps over the lazy dog. A sign containing his sentence is posted prominently near the ferry dock, where everyone sees it upon arrival. The island residents are highly literary, saying and writing witty things all the time, and when letters start falling off the sign, they are no longer able to use words containing the lost letters. It sounds strange, but the author is very creative; the characters start to speak and write phonetically, and the story doesn't suffer or lose momentum as the alphabet shrinks. An original idea and worth a re-read, this book appeals to all of us. Janelle plunks it into the nearest empty hand.

Due to her hiking and kayaking activities, Christine hasn't had time to read a book this past month, but she brought a word puzzle to the group. After she distributes a copy to each of us we sit and study the cryptic, haphazardly arranged random letters and numbers; suddenly a few answers appear, fully formed in my mind.

1. 26 L. of the A.
2. 9 D. in a S. S. N.
3. 88 P. K.
4. 13 S. on the A. F.
5. 32 D. at which W. F.
6. 18 H. on a G. C.
7. 90 D. in a R. A.
8. 8 S. on a S. S.
9. 4 Q. in a G.
10. 1 W. on a U.
11. 5 D. in a Z. C.
12. 11 P. on a F. T.
13. 29 D. in F. in a L. Y.
14. 64 S. on a C.
15. 54 C. in a D. (with J.)
16. 360 D. in a C.
17. 100 Y. in a C.

18. 3 B. M. (S. H. T. R.)
19. 1000 W. that a P. is W.
20. 200 D. for P. G. in M.
21. 16 O. in a P.

"Ooh! Twenty-six letters of the alphabet!" Jean calls out the first answer. After a chorus of chuckles, we start decoding phrases, enjoying the challenge, and Christine says she'll bring the answers to the next meeting. Pretty soon we're stumped, so we tuck the puzzles away and continue reviewing books.

Angie is presenting *The Opposite of Fate*, Amy Tan's compilation of meditations on her life, her career, her family, her illness, and her mother's death. This is the book's second appearance at a meeting, as I brought it last time; Angie and I agree it is Stamp-of-Approval-worthy, and deserving of shelf space. I will re-read it after it's made the rounds and is returned to me, but this time I'll be armed with Post-It notes to mark the best passages. A detailed review isn't required for any Amy Tan novel as she's earned her place on our Favorite Authors List, and this non-fictional collection of essays is eagerly accepted by Jean on faith. Angie finishes presenting and passing the remaining books in her stack, and nods at my mom to grant her the floor.

Mom brought Michael Perry's newest, a nonfiction story that reads like a novel, called *Truck: A Love Story*. She found it in the UP's finest bookstore, located in Marquette in a renovated house with several rooms of new and used books. The author lives in Eau Claire, Wisconsin, writing about the restoration of his beloved old Ford pickup truck and his adventures as a volunteer EMT on the local ambulance corps, and his introduction to and courtship of his wife. He's not a mechanic or an auto-body guy, merely using the sections about truck restoration as a central theme to tie the story together. Each chapter represents one month in this year-long tale. Besides writing books and patching up his friends and neighbors, Michael Perry has a great talent for song-writing and guitar-playing, and some of his performances provide the anecdotes appearing in his books. A delightful read featuring rural humor about small town happenings, Perry befriends the reader as he shares his life; somewhere between the slow healing of his truck and his tales of fellow EMTs, he charms us. We all want to meet the author, to hear him sing his songs and play his guitar.

The sun is starting to slip over the horizon as Mom finishes her review, so we hastily schedule a date for our next meeting and stow our books in tote bags to trundle out to our trucks. The evening air is cool and crisp, full of Autumn's clarity, with no allusion to the coming winter. When I arrive home, I shuffle my books several times before settling on a suitable reading order, cracking open the first one and allowing it to envelop me.

Christine's Menu

Butternut Squash Soup*

Cabbage & Apple Salad*

Blueberry Pound Cake*

Coffee * Cabernet Sauvignon * Chablis * Ice Water

*recipes included in Appendix C

"Does this thing have spell-check?"

Chapter Eight

On a typical day, a Wednesday, a day nowhere near any sort of anniversary, birthday, milestone or holiday, my husband Jason brought a brand new set of women's golf clubs home. "These are for you," he explained, with his typical brevity. Now, I'm no athlete; I consider reading outside to be a sport, I frequently trip on my own feet when walking, and I have a tendency to lose my balance sometimes when I'm standing with both feet planted firmly on a perfectly flat surface. *Golf clubs.*

The game of golf recently piqued my interest; my daughter had chosen golf as a high school sport and I was learning through her about the complicated rules, the strict etiquette, the dress code, the order of operations. She began playing golf to spend more time with her boyfriend, and I expected her interest to wane quickly. I was wrong, however; she started to watch golf on television, explaining everything to me over the whispered voice of the announcer, and she played in several golf meets across the UP, placing in a few of them. Impressed by her golf knowledge and increasing skill, I considered trying it but was reluctant to buy my own clubs.

My husband saw golf as a hobby we could enjoy together, requiring basic fitness but no great talent or upper body strength. We first attacked a nine-hole course, and though I didn't keep score, I think I did pretty well. Jason, a former hockey player in the Junior division, is a natural golfer. He frequently uses two golf balls and competes against himself, in an attempt to maintain my slow pace. A patient coach, he corrects my posture, comments on my follow through (either way too enthusiastic, or completely lacking), and never tires of letting me swing again when I miss the ball. We are frugal golfers, renting hand carts rather than driving carts, which is both fiscally and physically efficient, as my strokes are often appallingly short. With a hand cart, I quickly jog to the ball and hit it again. If I calculated the green fees as a ratio of strokes per dollar, I'd be getting a bargain!

Playing golf allows me to consider myself a 'true' athlete: I play a sport! I'm someone who chooses the right club for each stroke, who never casts her shadow upon the green while someone is putting and strides confidently toward the ball to hit it again (and then again), first extricating it from between the roots of a tree or retrieving it from a creek. During my brief exposure to golf society, I noticed even fairly competent golfers searching for their ball. I pretend my inaccuracy is a sudden development as we carefully inspect the woods and weeds for my elusive ball.

We make golf our own; the game that was originally an acronym for Gentlemen Only, Ladies Forbidden, now means Go On, Look Further. Searching for the ball, while challenging and occasionally rewarding (I usually find more than I lose), can be the worst part of the game. Carrying several extras prevents me from losing my mind on a ball-reconnaissance mission.

This autumn graced us with four weeks of beautiful weather, luring us to the golf course more often than usual. One of our frugal strategies is to golf after Labor Day, enjoying empty courses and lower prices, with weather more enjoyable than summer's humidity. The caveats to this strategy are few: the course isn't as lush, the hand carts a little wobbly from the seasonal use, and the evenings are shorter as we descend into winter, leaving us less time on a work day to wedge a round of golf into our schedules. The animals realize summer's busy time is over, as well: we occasionally catch deer grazing on the fairway, rabbits and squirrels are scampering about, and even the tourists have fled to warmer climes.

I haven't yet determined how to combine golf with reading; I'm sure there's a way, especially if one rents a cart and lets her partner drive. For now, I enjoy the outside interlude for what it is: a great date with my husband, a brief respite for my eyes, and a much-needed stretch for my legs. Exercising like this allows me to relax with a book, guilt free, when we return home.

∾

Colorful leaves drift off the trees to skip and dance along the roads in a spirited autumnal celebration; Mother Nature's ticker tape parade, the leaves offer a last salute to summer. Winter is looming, its cold, steely breath chilling our faces and hands in the early mornings and late evenings. The snow has yet to debut and the sun is still friendly in the afternoons, lifting our spirits as it bestows us with a spectacular sunset each night.

Once again, it's my turn to host Bookworms; I've created a theme menu around the lad of the hour, our guest of honor, my nephew Tucker. I'll serve Shrimp Appetizers, Baby Spinach Salad, and Leeky Soup. For dessert, we'll have Oatmeal Cake with Coconut Topping. The soup will feature wild leeks picked last spring, waiting in the freezer for this occasion. Leek season generally lasts two weeks each spring, when they push through the earth in riotous frenzies, waving their green, leafy flags to attract our attention. We corral them in a basket and carry them home, their earthy onion scent inspiring us to make leek tarts, leek soups, leek salads, and leek wine (I haven't tried this last one yet, but it sounds intriguing).

Devoting the day to Bookworm meeting preparation, I've assigned my daughter to create a seasonal centerpiece. She amassed a stylish collection of sticks and twigs, artfully arranged in a cut-crystal vase. We tied a colorful ribbon around each rolled cloth napkin, tucking a tiny three-twig bouquet in each one, and set the table with our almost-matching collection of white plates, and decidedly mismatching collection of water and wine glasses. A stack of paper plates and napkins, both featuring a blue baby-size footprint in the middle, are standing ready for dessert. My daughter is staying this evening to assist with Tucker management, as his interest tends to wane during adult conversations.

As the Bookworms arrive, the sun is weakening and heading toward the horizon; the scent of rotting leaves begs one to inhale large amounts of autumn evening air. If only we could preserve this air, and enjoy it when winter's influence is strongest! Everyone arrives at once, toting their bags of books, commenting on the centerpiece and fastidiously tied napkins, greeting Tucker and exclaiming over his bright, intelligent eyes and his resemblance to both parents. Jen has been reading to him, coaching him to refrain from chewing on books, showing him how to turn pages and point to pictures.

We settle around the table and start eating, briefing each other on our individual activities and personal victories. Jean's lead part in the play was a raving success, and she will consider acting in another play next year. Angie is the president of our Friends of the Library, and she announces upcoming events and developments at the library. Christine recently kayaked parts of Lake Superior with a group of friends and she's planning one last short paddle on the Au Train River before the winter weather arrives. Janelle illustrated a recently published children's book, telling us about working with the author and the unique packaging they chose—the title character is a teddy bear, so they are including one with each book they sell. My mom has been busy working in the store (she's a clerk for Timberdoodle), and gearing up for the night classes she teaches to help people earn their high school diplomas. Jen, of course, is busy with Tucker, trying to find time to read a word let alone an entire book, and I have been golfing, working, and reading. Our stacks of books aren't towering this evening, but each of us has at least three books ready to swap.

Some of tonight's books are:

Whistling in the Dark, by Lesley Kegan
Church of the Dog, by Kaya McLaren
Bee Season, by Myla Goldberg
We Were the Mulvaneys, by Joyce Carol Oates
Water for Elephants, by Sara Gruen
Skeletons at the Feast, by Chris Bohjalian

By the time dessert is finished and coffee is poured, we're through discussing current events and ready to address the books. Janelle begins tonight because she has a gift for each of us: she painted a watercolor scene on long, skinny paper, then cut it into strips so we each have a bookmark. If we put our bookmarks together in the proper order, we can view the entire scene, a landscape of trees in winter with a spectacular sky background. Janelle starts reviewing her first book, *Whistling in the Dark*, "This one takes place during the 1950's in Milwaukee, told by a 10-year-old girl who roams around the neighborhood with her younger sister, visiting neighbors and doing some light investigative work to find out who murdered two girls in her community. Her name is Sally O'Malley, and since her mother is in the hospital and her stepdad is a drunk, she's pretty much on her own. She's wise for her years and has some great lines—I discovered that life wasn't innocent in the late 50's, it was just that people didn't discuss things. Today people are more open about abuse and neglect." This is the book's third appearance at a meeting, so the three of us who have already read it urge the remaining members to take it. Angie tucks it in her bag.

Since Angie is sitting on Janelle's left, she takes her turn: "I brought three books tonight, but I don't think any of you will like any of them. I'll start with this one, which I took with me to the dermatologist's office because I'm always stuck waiting in the examining room. It seems like I'm there for 15 or 20 minutes before the doctor deigns to appear, and he always asks me what I'm reading. Apparently not many patients carry books with them, but I can't imagine what else they do while they're waiting in that room—there are no windows, and the magazines they provide are substandard at best. Anyway, at my last appointment, he gave me this book," she holds up another book, some sort of memoir, "and it's terrible. I hate it when people give me books that are bad, because they'll inevitably ask me if I enjoyed the book and I'll be forced to lie. It takes place in Michigan, so that kept me going, but the author is older than my dermatologist; he grew up in the area, and talks about local events and towns, but I don't know how many copies he'll sell." She pauses, considering, "Maybe that's why the dermatologist is giving them away!" Angie chuckles and retrieves her last book, continuing, "The third book I have is another documentary-style book. I don't know why I kept reading it, and I'm sure no one here will want it, but I brought it to show you just in case. And I need books! I need to take some good books home tonight." She stows her books in her bag and grants Jean the floor.

Living the life of an actress, enjoying more local celebrity than usual, Jean hasn't had much time to read. She finished *Skeletons at the Feast*, though, so she begins, "This was a good book, if you like the holocaust." We all chuckle around the table, wondering who in the world *likes* the holocaust. "This book read like a movie! We've got a Scottish soldier hiding in the wagon, a love interest between him and the daughter of the family…a Jewish refugee that appears at the most opportune times…I have cast Brad Pitt in one of the lead roles; I can visualize this entire plot on the big screen. They won't even have to rewrite it for the actors! It's already in script form." She's grinning, waving an arm around as if directing Mr. Pitt and his fellow actors on stage.

I jump in to defend the book, as it's written by one of my favorite authors, "I didn't see the movie aspect of this story; it contains horrible descriptions of the concentration camps and the women marching toward certain death, but the Scottish soldier and the Jewish refugee were interesting. Before the war arrived on their doorstep, the husband was chastised for heiling Hitler with a cavalier attitude while on a public street. Wealthy landowners on land that was previously Russian, the family clearly believed themselves beyond Hitler's reach, but the war found them and forced them to make some hard choices and adjustments." Christine is intrigued by the historical aspect of the book as well as the different reactions Jean and I shared; she takes the book, promising to read it first and try to forget about the Brad Pitt thing so she can form her own opinion.

Jean presents the rest of the books in her stack and gestures to Christine; Christine picks up her first book, holding it aloft so we can all view the cover, and says, "This is one screwed up family! I loved reading this book—it has Judaism, Hare Krishna, spelling bees, insanity, obsession, compulsion. Absolutely everything is in here." The red cover of *Bee Season*, designed to look like an old grade school workbook, is compelling and Christine's enthusiastic review somehow causes my hand to reach out and grab the book.

Janelle has read this one before, and she adds, "The daughter in the story, I think her name is Eliza, was completely overlooked by the parents; the father was always trying to commune with God, the mother was preoccupied by her own mad compulsions, and the brother Aaron was the father's favorite child and main focus, besides God. When Eliza started winning spelling bees, no one in the family knew how to deal with her success, and things just fell apart. It's a great read. The author's photo on the back is what sold me." I flip the book over to show everyone the author, quirky and intelligent, long legs showcased in black and white striped stockings.

My mom is next in our round robin, returning two books the rest of us have read and presenting an issue of Newsweek about education in America. She brought the entire magazine so we can each borrow it; a brief conversation follows about our local school, struggling with a lack of funds and a lack of students. Although we could solve all of these problems this evening, there are more books to review. We table the discussion and continue with Jen's review of *We Were the Mulvaneys*.

"This one is also about a family that kind of falls apart," Jen balances Tucker with one arm and holds the book out of his reach, continuing, "it takes place in the 1960's, so you have to keep that in mind; the family has three sons and one daughter, and they are highly respected in their small community. When the daughter gets into a date-rape situation, the family is shunned. It seems crazy, but the assaulter's family just goes on as usual and this respectable, dignified family falls completely apart. The two older sons take off, one to Vietnam, one to an Ivy League school, and the youngest son is the narrator. The daughter goes to this hippie commune and eventually gets herself together; the mother just stands by while her husband drinks himself to death, and then she reconnects with her daughter." She glances around the table and sees we've all read this one, so she checks for a name inside the front cover and hands it back to Jean. If any Joyce Carol Oates book deserves the Bookworm Stamp of Approval, it is this one. We're not Oates fans, but sometimes she cranks out a compelling book we all enjoy.

It's my turn to review; I'm starting with a fun, uplifting story about an old farm couple, Earl and Edith, who rent housing quarters in their barn to a young, flighty art teacher who believes in auras and visits people in her dreams. Mara, the art teacher, paints a mural of a dog on the side of the barn, and a few nights later a dog shows up. He looks uncannily like her portrait, so she adopts him and names him Zeus. Earl teaches Mara how to dance, Mara takes Edith on midnight excursions on horseback, and Earl and Edith rekindle their marriage. *Church of the Dog* is about positive thinking, not getting mired in the details, and making life fun whenever possible. It's short and reads fast, two features attractive to everyone. I hand it off to Jen as it's the perfect size for reading while rocking the baby. Tucker has spent the evening on Jen's lap, content to watch and listen, our first student of the book club.

The hour is late when I finish the remaining books in my stack. We schedule our next meeting, wondering if we'll be tramping through the snow by then. As everyone files out the door, I clear the table and pour myself the last glass of wine, curl into the reading position, and start on page one.

Jan's Menu

Shrimp Appetizers*

Baby Spinach Salad

Leeky Soup*

Oatmeal Cake w/ Coconut Topping*

Coffee* Merlot* Pinot Grigio* Ice Water

*recipes included in Appendix C

Enjoy yourself! It's later than you think…

Epilogue

● ● ●

Auctions, garage sales, and recycling (i.e., leaving old, yet still useful, stuff in the recycling shack for someone else to take home and use) have always been popular Upper Peninsula fair weather activities. Winter's imminence effectively terminates garage sale season, when people survey their basements or garages and notice the piles of clutter collecting dust. They consult the calendar and calculate the number of months it will continue to collect dust if they outwait the winter before holding a panic-induced garage sale. These last minute sales are the best ones, featuring chaotic displays and extremely low prices. The amateur garage saler can easily capitalize on the owner's anxiety, negotiating to drop the already low prices to an embarrassing level. Garage saling is an unrecognized sport, incorporating budgeting, route planning, neighborhood demographic research, scheduling, and transportation preparation (cleaning out the truck to cart the new treasures home).

Invariably, a rickety table supports piles of books, mainly Harlequin romances and college texts from the 1970's, but occasionally a seasoned book junkie or highly trained garage saler can unearth one or two books worth reading. I usually approach the book table with trepidation, low expectations firmly established, yet unable to relinquish the search for intriguing titles. As I browse, sorting and rearranging the books into some logical order, I notice my expectations sinking to a subterranean level, thereby decreasing my book-buying standards with alarming efficiency. After gazing at so many third rate titles, the new lower standard suddenly causes me to consider a manual about preparing homemade cat food appealing; after all, it's better than the nearby volumes about camping in the Rocky Mountains or learning to write FORTRAN computer programs in nine easy lessons. I'm compelled to rescue some of these imminently homeless books; the urge to purchase a book whenever one is passed before my face is difficult to control, even in the best circumstances; I realize I've chosen an orphaned book, cradling it while I browse the remaining castoff items, then return to reality and abandon the unreadable paperback for some outdated eye shadow or unattractive costume jewelry. It's disturbing to think about them as I leave the sale— surely someone can use a repair manual for all air conditioners manufactured between 1972 and 1979; surely they won't suffer a cruel death, rotting slowly in a landfill or burning in a backyard fire pit/crematorium. Maybe they could be sold on Ebay...

∽

Bookworms Anonymous, with its deep friendship, easy camaraderie, boisterous laughter and witty conversations, changed the way I manage my reading habit. As I've said before, this type of book club offers many benefits traditional book clubs lack, the most obvious being freedom to choose what I read and no schedule within which to read it. I enjoy a more enriching reading experience, paying closer attention to the story and characters, marking the occasional passage with a Post-It note or jotting down a couple of words to effectively encapsulate the plot, preparing for my presentation to the group.

I've read many books I never would have found had they not been touted by a fellow Bookworm; garage sale pressure notwithstanding, my taste in literature has evolved. I've become a highly selective book snob, browsing the Literature section of the bookstore, seeking books featuring artful phrasing rather than the pedestrian prose found in the Popular Fiction section. I'm also saving money—each Bookworm can buy as many or as few books as she pleases, with special recognition for one who finds a quality title at a garage sale or thrift store. Our loose meeting format also allows for other literature-related materials, such as magazine articles or word puzzles, so we're not limited to full-length books. My favorite feature is the lack of dissection: we don't discuss theme, style, or intent. We simply read, meet, eat, and repeat.

My method of book management has been modified and improved: prior to Bookworms Anonymous, I saved every book I purchased; my permanent collection resided haphazardly on several overloaded bookcases in awkward stacks and piles, lacking subject organization and alphabetization. I still frequent bookstores, rarely leaving without a significant purchase, but few books merit placement in my permanent collection; they join my temporary collection, revolving from Bookworm to Bookworm, purchased with the objective to read, share, and donate. Making a purchase without intending long term ownership allows me to enjoy the book for what it is: a short-term source of entertainment, without the shelf space commitment.

Technology has invaded literary society, in the form of a slim, page-sized computer, benign appearance belying its capacity for several hundred books, eliminating the need for shelf space and providing the reader control of font size and screen contrast, to reduce eye fatigue. The per-title cost is less than the average 'real' book; titles can be shared with five or six friends, and arranged in any order, facilitating the book swapping and book shuffling processes.

So, how far is technology going to carry (or bury) us? Will traditional books be phased out, and readers forced to shop exclusively online for electronic files, free from the influence of fresh ink scent or cover art appeal? Will our bookshelves host only dusty antique volumes, curious samples of an abandoned pastime, worthy of museum display? If so, what will become of societies such as Bookworms Anonymous? Technology's inexorable progress will force us to surrender our traditional reading habits, and we'll each own an electronic reading device. If conventional books cease to exist, will we simply beam our book files to each other, allowing our book club to expire? Such a device might be best employed by reading periodicals, facilitating immediate delivery of each issue and reducing waste, but if the electronic device replaces real books, I hope I don't witness it. Life after books conjures visions of a desperate, repugnant existence.

And yet, maybe it isn't about the books. Maybe the real reason our Bookworms Anonymous group has retained its fresh glow over the years is the sheer simplicity of the model: friends gathering together around a table, sharing food and insights, helping each other weave richer, more interesting patterns through our lives. The books are just the common threads, holding us together.

Appendix A:

Opening a Chapter of Bookworms Anonymous

Bookworms are the most important elements of any Bookworms Anonymous chapter. Determining whom to invite to the first meeting is critical to the success of the meetings and the longevity of the group—consider individual reading interests as well as personality types, to ensure a pleasant chemistry within the group. Below is a list of some characteristics the perfect Bookworm might possess:

* Avid Readers—this sounds obvious, but with no books, there are no Bookworms!
* Open-Minded Readers—BA members should be ready and willing to try books they wouldn't normally read, to expand their reading repertoire.
* Chatty Cathys—Conversation is one of the best parts of a meeting! Choose people who will keep it moving.
* Good Cooks—Or, at least, creative frozen food preparers!
* Frugal, yet Generous People—Readers who enjoy finding a great deal on a book, and sharing it with each other. Most Bookworms rank books directly below the mortgage in their budgets, willing to eat leftovers and wear old shoes to afford more books.

* Conscientious Book Handlers—Page benders and binding busters will require remedial training to adopt appropriate book handling habits.
* Dedicated People—Commitment-phobic readers will cause the Chapter to expire early.
* Readers who Prioritize Properly—Reading at every opportunity, even at the expense of household chores or dinner preparation, is not only acceptable, it's expected behavior for a true Bookworm.

Friends make great fellow Bookworms; however, if the entire Chapter consists of members involved in each other's daily lives, the conversation will lag at meetings. Everyone will already know everyone else's current status, what they're reading, where they're vacationing, and what they did last night. Another problem with daily friends being fellow Bookworms is the tendency to swap books outside the Bookworm venue—when that starts happening, it's tempting to postpone a meeting, then cancel it, eventually terminating the Chapter altogether.

Start with personal friends, and find out if they have coworkers or friends from other social circles who fit the Bookworm description. It should be fairly easy to find five or six people interested in joining a reading group; if you need more members, try meeting in a coffee house or bookstore and see if any passersby are intrigued by your discussions.

An afternoon tea or simple cocktail party makes a great kick-off meeting; potential members gather, chat about the meeting format and bring one or two favorite books to share. During the first few meetings, conversation may be somewhat stilted and book swapping tentative; don't be discouraged! After meeting several times and adjusting to everyone's reading preferences and personality styles, the meetings will morph into the boisterous gatherings filled with witty remarks and wild laughter we Charter Member Bookworms enjoy.

Once the new Chapter of Bookworms Anonymous is established, some members may want to journal the meetings; a sample journal page is provided at the end of Appendix A. It's amazing how difficult it is to remember which books were favorites or what everyone served to eat, and it's interesting to record sideline facts such as weather or notes about conversations. A comfortable routine will quickly emerge, in which hosting order is determined and favorite authors and titles acknowledged. The journal pages provided here can be photocopied and kept in a binder, or the information can be recorded in a notebook during or after each meeting.

Remember, life's too short to read bad books. Keep it enjoyable and fun—read, eat, meet, repeat.

Bookworms Anonymous Journal

Meeting Date:

Hostess:

Attendees:

Menu:

Weather:

Books Brought to Meeting:

Books Taken from Meeting:

Notes:

Form also available on www.bookwormsanonymous.com

Appendix B:

Books That Earned the Bookworms Anonymous Stamp of Approval:

(in alphabetical order by author's last name)

Saving the World, by Julia Alverez
Midnight Champagne, by A. Manette Ansay
Handmaid's Tale, by Margaret Atwood
The Robber Bride, by Margaret Atwood
The Girls' Guide to Hunting and Fishing, by Melissa Bank
The Clothes They Stood Up In, by Alan Bennett
Those Who Save Us, by Jenna Blum
Midwives, by Chris Bohjalian
The Buffalo Soldier, by Chris Bohjalian
Girl with a Pearl Earring, by Tracy Chevalier
The Loop, by Joe Coomer
The Madonnas of Leningrad, by Debra Dean
The Red Tent, by Anita Diamant
The Whistling Season, by Ivan Doig
Ella Minnow Pea, by Mark Dunn
The Turtle Warrior, by Mary Ellis
The Last Report on the Miracles at Little No Horse, by Louise Erdrich
The Master Butcher's Singing Club, by Louise Erdrich
The Painted Drum, by Louise Erdrich
Middlesex, by Jeffrey Eugenides
A Thousand White Women, by Jim Fergus

The Jane Austen Book Club, by Karen Joy Fowler
The Corrections, by Jonathan Franzen
Charms For an Easy Life, by Kaye Gibbons
Wild Life, by Molly Gloss
Bee Season, by Myla Goldberg
A Painted House, by John Grisham
The Monsters of Templeton, by Lauren Groff
Snow Falling on Cedars, by David Guterson
The Curious Incident of the Dog in the Nighttime, by Marc Haddon
Disobedience, by Jane Hamilton
Map of the World, by Jane Hamilton
The Short History of a Prince, by Jane Hamilton
The Road Home, by Jim Harrison
Stones From the River, by Ursula Hegi
Empress of the Splendid Season, by Oscar Hijuelos
The Kite Runner, by Khaled Hosseini
A Prayer for Owen Meany, by John Irving
The World According to Garp, by John Irving
Whistling in the Dark, by Lesley Kegan
The Poisonwood Bible, by Barbara Kingsolver
Prodigal Summer, by Barbara Kingsolver
The Namesake, by Jhumpa Lahiri
The Hour I First Believed, by Wally Lamb
I Know This Much Is True, by Wally Lamb
In the Fall, by Jeffrey Lent
Where the Heart Is, by Billie Letts
The Last Chinese Chef, by Nicole Mones
The Center of Everything, by Laura Moriarty
It Takes a Village Idiot, by Jim Mullen
Abundance, by Sena Jeter Naslund
Ahab's Wife, by Sena Jeter Naslund
We Were the Mulvaneys, by Joyce Carol Oates

The Magician's Assistant, by Ann Patchett
Run, by Ann Patchett
My Sister's Keeper, by Jodi Picoult
Lucy Crocker 2.0, by Caroline Preston
One True Thing, by Anna Quindlen
Bridge of Sighs, by Richard Russo
Empire Falls, by Richard Russo
Larry's Party, by Carol Shields
The Stone Diaries, by Carol Shields
Unless, by Carol Shields
The Radioactive Boy Scout, by Ken Silverstein
Big Rock Candy Mountain, by Wallace Stegner
Chang and Eng, by Darin Strauss
The Bonesetter's Daughter, by Amy Tan
The Opposite of Fate, by Amy Tan
The Accidental Tourist, by Anne Tyler
The Miracle Life of Edgar Mint, by Brady Udall
Lottery, by Patricia Wood
The Story of Edgar Sawtelle, by David Wroblewski

Appendix C:
The Recipes

A meeting without food is like a gift without a ribbon.

Jan's Lentil Pate

- 1 cup lentils, pre-cooked in
  2 cups water OR 1-1/2 cups
  canned cooked lentils drained
- 1 sweet onion, chopped
- 4 cloves garlic, minced

- 6 teaspoons margarine
- 1 teaspoon black pepper
- Water if necessary
- 1/2 teaspoon vinegar

In a large saucepan, gently saute sweet onion and garlic in the margarine over low heat until soft, but not browned. Season with black pepper. Add lentils and heat until warmed through. Scrape lentil mixture into the bowl of a food processor fitted with the metal chopping blade. Process until smooth, adding water if necessary. Add vinegar and pulse until combined. Serve lentil pate at room temperature with toasted bread rounds or savory crackers for a delicious vegetarian appetizer appealing to all.

Jan's Spinach Ricotta Tart

- 1 (17.3 oz) pkg frozen puff pastry sheets, thawed
- 1 large egg, beaten with 1 teaspoon water
- 1/3 cup grated Parmesan cheese, divided
- 1 (15 oz) container ricotta cheese (small curd cottage cheese will work)
- 2 Tablespoons extra virgin olive oil
- 1 large egg, lightly beaten
- ¼ teaspoon salt
- ¼ teaspoon freshly ground pepper
- ¼ teaspoon ground nutmeg
- 12 ounces fresh spinach (frozen can be used in a pinch)
- 1 cup sliced mushrooms, optional
- Purple onion, sliced into thin rings

Preheat oven to 350 degrees. Unfold one pastry sheet, pinching seams together if necessary, and place onto 10" x 15" clay baking sheet. Trim second pastry sheet into 4 strips and use for borders on bottom layer. Brush with egg wash; sprinkle with salt and Parmesan cheese. Prick bottom sheet several times with fork. Sprinkle half of Parmesan cheese over bottom; place on lower rack of oven and bake for 5-8 minutes or until cheese forms a slight crust. Let cool for five minutes. Sauté the mushrooms and spinach over medium high heat. Spread about 2/3 of the cheese mixture over the crust; spread the spinach and mushrooms as evenly as possible over the cheese. Dollop the rest of the cheese on top of the spinach, then arrange onion rings on top. Sprinkle with the rest of the Parmesan cheese. Bake for 15-18 minutes, until slightly browned. Let sit five minutes before cutting and serving.

Jan's Walnut-Stuffed Slow-Baked Apples

- ½ cup coarsely chopped walnuts
- ½ cup dried cranberries
- ¼ cup brown sugar
- 1 ½ teaspoons ground cinnamon, divided

- 8 large Granny Smith apples, cored
- 1 ½ cups packed brown sugar
- 1 ½ cups apple cider

Combine first three ingredients; add ½ teaspoon cinnamon, stirring to mix well. Peel top third of each apple; place apples in 9" x 13" pan. Spoon walnut mixture into cavity of each apple. Combine the remaining teaspoon cinnamon, 1 ½ cups brown sugar and apple cider in a small bowl, stirring to blend. Pour over apples. Cover tightly with aluminum foil and bake at 170 degrees 2 hours. Remove the apples with a slotted spoon. Spoon ¼ cup cooked cider mixture over each serving. Serve these apples warm from the oven with whipped topping or frozen yogurt.

Anne's Mozzarella Tomato Basil Salad

- 8 ounces mozzarella cheese, cut into cubes
- 1/3 cup olive oil
- ½ cup fresh basil, chopped
- 1 Tablespoon fresh dill, chopped
- salt and pepper to taste
- 1 pint cherry or grape tomatoes, halved

Combine cheese, olive oil, herbs, salt, and pepper. Refrigerate over night. Add tomatoes just before serving.

Anne's Lentil Casserole

- 1 cup dried lentils
- 3 cups water
- 1 large yellow onion, chopped
- 2 carrots, chopped
- ½ cup diced celery
- 2 cloves garlic, minced
- Olive oil
- 1 teaspoon mixed dried herbs
- 1-15oz can petite diced tomatoes
- 2 Tablespoons soy sauce
- 2 Tablespoons chopped parsley
- Salt
- Freshly ground pepper
- Biscuit mix (a cornmeal Jiffy mix works great)
- Dried, minced onions (optional)
- Paprika

Boil lentils 45 minutes; drain. Preheat oven to 350°. Saute onion, carrots, celery, and garlic in oil until soft. Add herbs, tomatoes, soy sauce, lentils, parsley, salt and pepper to taste. Stir and spoon into greased 9"x13" baking dish. Spread with biscuit dough or cornmeal muffin dough. Sprinkle with dried, minced onions if using, and paprika. Bake 45 minutes.

Anne's Cream Cheese Cookies

- 1 cup butter, softened
- 6 ounces cream cheese, softened
- 1 cup granulated sugar
- 1 teaspoon vanilla

- 2 cups sifted flour
- 1 Tablespoon baking powder
- ¼ teaspoon salt
- 1 cup oatmeal
- ½ chopped walnuts

Beat together butter and cream cheese until creamy. Add sugar and vanilla; beat again. Sift together flour, baking powder and salt. Add to creamed mixture. Stir in oatmeal and walnuts. Mix well. Chill several hours. Roll into balls, then roll in flour. Bake at 350° 12 to 15 minutes.

Jenny Penny's Vegetarian Chili

- 1-32 oz pkg. veggie crumbles (soy-based meat substitute)
- 1-29 oz can tomato sauce
- 1-29 oz can diced tomatoes
- 2-15 oz can Brooks chili beans (1 hot, 1 mild)
- 1 fresh tomato, diced
- 2 Tablespoons diced jalapenos
- 1 clove garlic, minced
- 1 teaspoon bay leaves (or 2 whole bay leaves)
- 1 Tablespoon sugar
- 3-4 Tablespoons chili powder
- Freshly ground pepper to taste

Dump everything in crock pot; cook on low for 6 hours. Serve.

Jen's Apricot Whip

- 1 ½ cups dried apricots
  Boiling water
- 1 ½ cups plain yogurt
- 2 Tablespoons honey
- 2 Tablespoons finely chopped pecans

Pour boiling water over apricots and soak for about thirty minutes. Drain and combine the apricots with the other ingredients in a food processor. Process until a smooth consistency is reached. Chill and serve with pecans sprinkled over each serving.

Jean's Lasagne

- 1 Tablespoon olive oil
- 2-10 oz pkgs frozen chopped spinach
- ½ onion, chopped
- ½ teaspoon dried oregano
- ½ teaspoon dried basil
- 2 cloves garlic, crushed
- 1-32 oz jar spaghetti sauce
- 1 ½ cups water
- 2 cups non-fat cottage cheese
- 1-8 oz pkg mozzarella cheese, shredded
- ¼ cup grated Parmesan cheese
- ½ cup fresh parsley, chopped
- 1 teaspoon salt
- freshly ground pepper, to taste
- 1 egg
- 8 oz lasagne noodles

Preheat oven to 350° F (175° C). In a large pot over medium heat saute spinach, onion, oregano, basil and garlic in the olive oil. Pour in spaghetti sauce and water; simmer 20 minutes. In a large bowl mix cottage cheese, mozzarella cheese, Parmesan cheese, parsley, salt, pepper and egg. Place a small amount of sauce in the bottom of a 9" x 12" pan. Place 4 uncooked noodles on top of sauce and top with layer of sauce. Add 4 more noodles and layer with 1/2 sauce and 1/2 cheese mixture, and repeat layers until all is layered, finishing with sauce. Cover with foil and bake in a preheated oven for 55 minutes. Remove foil and bake another 15 minutes. Let sit 10 minutes before serving.

Jean's Berry Pie

Use a pre-made pie crust, or make it ahead (Jean makes hers from scratch). Bake as directed and cool.

- 4 cups blueberries and/or strawberries, divided
- 3 Tablespoons cornstarch
- 1 cup sugar
- 1 cup water
- juice of 1/2 lemon

Cook 2 cups of the berries and all other ingredients until thick. Add the remaining 2 cups of berries; cool entire mixture and pour into pie crust. Chill in refrigerator for at least an hour. Serve with cool whip.

Angie's Enlightened Waldorf Salad

- 3 Pink Lady apples, cored and diced
- 3 Granny Smith apples, cored and diced
- 6-8 stalks celery, diced
- ½ cup dried cherries or cranberries

- 1 cup toasted walnuts
- 2 Tablespoons walnut oil
- 1 Tablespoon cider vinegar
- ½ teaspoon salt
- ½ teaspoon pepper

Toss together the apples, celery, dried cherries or cranberries, and walnuts in a large bowl; set aside. In a small bowl, whisk together the walnut oil, cider vinegar, salt, and pepper. Toss the apples with the dressing to serve. Leftovers are still good the next day or two when stored covered in refrigerator.

Angie's Cauliflower Pepper Salad

- 1 cauliflower
- 2 green bell peppers, diced
- 2 yellow bell peppers, diced
- 2 red bell peppers, diced
- ½ cup olive oil
- ¼ cup vinegar
- 2 cloves garlic
- ½ teaspoon oregano
- Salt and pepper

Separate cauliflower into fleurettes and soak in water and vinegar for 10 minutes. Cook in boiling water for 10 minutes. Cauliflower should be crisp. Season with salt, pepper and vinegar. Chill. Add diced peppers and season with olive oil, garlic, salt, pepper and oregano. Toss with dressing and serve.

Dressing:
- 1 Tablespoon Dijon mustard
- ¼ cup vinegar or lemon juice
- ½ cup finely sliced green onions
- 1 cup olive oil
- Salt and pepper, to taste

Mix together; pour over salad.

Angie's Sweet & Sour Bean Salad

- 1 15-oz. can cut green beans, drained
- 1 15-oz. can cut yellow beans, drained
- 1 16-oz. can kidney beans, drained
- ½ cup chopped bell pepper (both red and green if possible)
- ½ cup finely chopped sweet or purple onion

Dressing:
- ½ cup vegetable oil
- ½ cup cider vinegar
- 1 teaspoon salt
- ½ teaspoon ground pepper
- 1/3 cup sugar

Place beans and chopped vegetables in a serving bowl. Whisk together the dressing ingredients; pour over vegetables. Toss to coat well. Cover and refrigerate overnight or at least 8 hours.

Angie's Biscotti

- 1½ cups flour
- ¾ cup sugar
- ¾ cup oats, uncooked
- 2 Tablespoons yellow cornmeal
- 1 teaspoon baking powder
- ½ teaspoon cinnamon
- 1/8 teaspoon salt
- 2 large eggs, lightly beaten
- ¼ cup butter, melted
- 1 teaspoon butter
- 1 teaspoon vanilla or maple flavoring
- ½ cup chopped nuts (walnuts, pecans)
- ½ cup dried fruit (cherries, cranberries, raisins)

Preheat oven at 350°. Combine flour, sugar, oats, cornmeal, baking powder, cinnamon, and salt. Stir in eggs, butter, and vanilla. Also stir in nuts or dried fruit if desired. Divide dough into 2 logs. Bake for 25 minutes. Cut into diagonal slices 1/2 to 1 inch thick. Bake again for 6-9 minutes. Cool; serve.

Janelle's Asian Slaw & Brenda's Ginger Dressing

- 4 cups Napa cabbage, sliced thin
- 1 cup purple cabbage, shredded
- 1 cup shredded carrots
- ½ cup prepared edamame (see package for preparation directions)
- ¼ cup toasted almonds
- 12 wonton wrappers (toasted until crisp on a cookie sheet in the oven)

Combine the first four ingredients and dress with your favorite ginger dressing (or use the recipe below).

Break up the toasted wonton wrappers and add right before serving. Grilled protein of your choice could be added to the top to make it into a meal (chicken, shrimp, etc).

Brenda's Ginger Dressing

I wish I could take credit for this, but it's a recipe my sister-in-law came up with and it is the BEST. The ingredients are hard to track down & usually require a trip "down below" to acquire some, but miso will last for months in your fridge and it is worth it. –Janelle

- 12 Tablespoons vegetable or safflower oil
- 6 Tablespoons rice vinegar
- 3 Tablespoons white Miso bean paste (comes in a tub from Asian market in produce section)
- 1 Tablespoon onion, chopped
- 2-4 Tablespoons fresh grated ginger
- 2-3 teaspoons low sodium soy sauce

Add to blender and mix. I tend to use the max amount of ginger, but it all depends on your taste.

Janelle's Spring Rolls

- 2 ounces rice vermicelli
- 8 rice wrappers (8.5 inch diameter)
- 12 large cooked shrimp, peeled, de-veined and cut in half
- 2-3 large romaine lettuce leaves, chopped
- 3 large carrots, cut into matchsticks
- 1 cucumber, peeled, deseeded and cut into matchsticks
- 1 cup fresh cilantro, washed and chopped
- ½ cup fresh mint (optional)

Bring a medium saucepan of water to boil. Boil rice vermicelli 3 to 5 minutes, or until al dente, and drain. Fill a pie plate with warm water. Dip one wrapper into the hot water for a few seconds to soften. Blot on a clean towel and lay wrapper flat. In a row across the center, place 3 shrimp halves, a handful of vermicelli, lettuce, carrots, cucumber, cilantro and mint, leaving about 2 inches uncovered on each side. Fold uncovered sides inward, then tightly roll the wrapper, beginning at the end with the lettuce. Repeat with remaining ingredients. Serve with small bowls of dipping sauce. Use the ginger dressing recipe above or buy a bottle of peanut sauce (House of Tsang makes a good one). In a quick pinch equal parts seasoned rice vinegar and soy sauce with just a drizzle of oil and garnished with green onion or chives works great and is tangy and light.

Janelle's Easiest Chocolate Cake EVER!!

- One box plain devil's food cake mix (no pudding)
- 10 oz diet soda (Faygo cream soda works well)

Mix well and pour into a cake pan sprayed with non stick spray and dusted with cocoa powder. Bake until a toothpick comes out clean (may take longer than the time given on the cake box).

Serve with fresh berries and whipped cream

Christine's Butternut Squash Soup

- Extra virgin olive oil
- 1 stick butter
- 1 or 2 large sweet onions, chopped
- ½ large fennel bulb with "fern"
- 1 large butternut squash

- 2 large carrots
- White wine or Zinfandel
- Fresh sage
- 4 large cans chicken broth (may use low sodium)
- Salt
- Pepper

Pour generous amount of olive oil to cover bottom of a stock pot. Add ¼- ½ stick butter. Heat over low-medium heat. Add chopped onion. Cook until translucent. Clean fennel bulb and the fern (the fern is the top, finely-leafed portion of the fennel) under cold water and pat dry. Detach some fern from stems, discarding stems (they can be pithy). Chop bulb, discarding tough outer layer. Add chopped fennel bulb to onion and continue to sauté over low heat, stirring occasionally. Peel squash and carrots. Cut squash into medium sized cubes; slice carrot. Add approximately 2 teaspoons salt to pan (Kosher salt preferred), and sprinkle with pepper (use white pepper if available). Turn heat to medium, add ¼-1 cup wine to onion and fennel; cook until alcohol "burns off", approximately 4 to 5 minutes. Add carrot and squash to pot. Add 4 or 5 cans of chicken stock and remaining butter. Cover and bring to a slow boil. Mince several sage leaves and chop reserved fennel fern. Add to pot. Reduce to simmer, and cook until vegetables are very tender. Flavor with a dash of cinnamon, cayenne pepper, curry powder, nutmeg, and ginger, if preferred. Remove soup from heat and puree with hand mixer/blender.

Christine's Cabbage and Apple Salad

- 2 Tablespoons red wine vinegar or balsamic vinegar
- 1 Tablespoon cider vinegar
- 1 Tablespoon honey
- 1 Tablespoon spicy mustard
- ¼ cup extra virgin olive oil
- 2 medium unpeeled Pink Lady or Honey Crisp apples, cored, quartered, and thinly sliced
- 2 Tablespoons fresh lemon juice
- 3 cups coarsely shredded red cabbage
- 2 cups coarsely shredded green cabbage
- ¾ cup dried cranberries or cherries
- ¾ cup pecan halves, toasted (optional)
- Salt
- Pepper

Whisk both vinegars and mustard in small bowl. Gradually whisk in the honey and olive oil. Toss apples with lemon juice, shredded cabbage, and dried cranberries. Add dressing and toss. Add salt and pepper, to taste. Stir in pecans, if using. Refrigerate salad and toss again before serving.

Christine's Blueberry Pound Cake

- 1 cup butter, softened
- 2 cups granulated sugar
- 4 eggs
- 1 teaspoon vanilla

- 3 cups flour, divided
- ½ teaspoon salt
- 1 teaspoon baking powder
- 1 pint fresh blueberries

Cream together butter and sugar. Beat in eggs, one at a time, until light and fluffy; add vanilla. Combine flour, salt and baking powder; beat into creamed mixture. Grease and flour bundt pan and fill with batter. Bake at 325° for an hour and 15 minutes or until toothpick comes out clean. Serve with ice cream and/or fresh berries.

Tucker's Shrimp Appetizers

- 2 cups shredded cheddar cheese
- ½ cup butter, softened
- 1 egg, separated
- 25-35 bread squares (I use a firm bread, such as multigrain or rye.)
- 25-35 shrimp, cooked, peeled and de-veined

Cream together the butter and cheese. Blend in egg yolk. In a separate bowl, beat egg white until stiff peaks form. Mix egg white into cheese mixture. Place the bread squares on an ungreased cookie sheet. Top each bread square with one shrimp and cover with rounded teaspoonful of the cheese mixture. Bake at 350° for about 15 minutes, or until golden brown. Serve hot.

Tucker's Leeky Soup

- 2 cups sliced leeks
- 2 Tablespoons butter
- 1 teaspoon sugar
- Freshly ground black pepper
- 4 ½ cups hot beef or vegetable boullion
- 1/3 loaf heavy bread, preferably whole grain, sliced thick
- 6 oz. Swiss cheese, thinly sliced
- 3 Tablespoons butter

Saute leeks in two tablespoons butter until transparent and fragrant. Sprinkle with sugar and pepper; add hot bouillon. Simmer ten minutes. Cut the bread slices in half and arrange them in a deep 9"x13" pan, or other deep ovenproof casserole dish. Top each slice of bread with a slice of cheese. Slowly pour the leek mixture over all. Dot with remaining butter and bake, uncovered, at 350° for 45-60 minutes.

Tucker's Oatmeal Cake
(Recipe provided by Janelle's mom, Pauline)

- 1 cup oats, quick or old-fashioned
- 1 ¼ cup lukewarm water
- 1 cup white granulated sugar
- 1 cup brown sugar
- ½ cup butter

- 2 eggs
- 1 1/3 cup flour
- ½ teaspoon salt
- 1 teaspoon baking soda
- 1 teaspoon cinnamon
- 1 teaspoon baking powder

Soak oatmeal in lukewarm water; set aside. Cream together the sugars, butter and eggs. In a separate bowl, sift together the flour, salt, baking soda, cinnamon and baking powder; add to creamed mixture and mix well. Stir in oatmeal mixture. Bake in greased 9"x13" pan for 30-40 minutes at 350°.

Topping:
- 1 ½ cups brown sugar
- ¾ cup butter
- 3 Tablespoons milk
- ¾ teaspoon vanilla
- 1 ½ cups shredded coconut
- 1 ½ cups walnuts or pecans (can substitute Rice Krispies cereal if desired)

In a saucepan on the stove, cook the brown sugar, butter and milk until bubbly, then add the remaining ingredients. Pour over hot cake as soon as it's done baking, then return to oven and broil for a few minutes.

Appendix D:

Word Puzzle Answers

1. 26 L. of the A.	26 Letters of the Alphabet
2. 9 D. in a S. S. N.	9 Digits in a Social Security Number
3. 88 P. K.	88 Piano Keys
4. 13 S. on the A. F.	13 Stripes on the American Flag
5. 32 D. at which W. F.	32 Degrees at which Water Freezes
6. 18 H. on a G. C.	18 Holes on a Golf Course
7. 90 D. in a R. A.	90 Degrees in a Right Angle
8. 8 S. on a S. S.	8 Sides on a Stop Sign
9. 4 Q. in a G.	4 Quarts in a Gallon
10. 1 W. on a U.	1 Wheel on a Unicycle
11. 5 D. in a Z. C.	5 Digits in a Zip Code
12. 11 P. on a F. T.	11 Players on a Football Team
13. 29 D. in F. in a L. Y.	29 Days in February in a Leap Year
14. 64 S. on a C.	64 Squares on a Checkerboard
15. 54 C. in a D. (with J.)	54 Cards in a Deck (with Jokers)
16. 360 D. in a C.	360 Degrees in a Circle
17. 100 Y. in a C.	100 Years in a Century

18. 3 B. M. (S. H. T. R.)   3 Blind Mice (See How They Run)

19. 1000 W. that a P. is W.   1000 Words that a Picture is Worth

20. 200 D. for P. G. in M.   200 Dollars for Passing Go in Monopoly

21. 16 O. in a P.   16 Ounces in a Pint

About the Author

Jan Kellis lives in Michigan's Upper Peninsula with her husband Jason, daughter Stephanie, and chocolate lab, Spirit. She works full time for an electric utility company and maintains a gourmet food line of products at the Timberdoodle Mercantile, carving out reading and writing time whenever possible. Visit her website, www.bookwormsanonymous.com, for more information.

Made in the USA